TERENCE RILEY The Un-Private House

TERENCE RILEY

The Un-Private House

THE MUSEUM OF MODERN ART, NEW YORK
DISTRIBUTED BY HARRY N. ABRAMS, INC., NEW YORK

Published on the occasion of the exhibition *The Un-Private House*, organized by Terence Riley, Chief Curator, Department of Architecture and Design, The Museum of Modern Art, New York, July 1–October 5, 1999.

The exhibition is made possible by The Lily Auchincloss Fund for Contemporary Architecture, and is the first in a series of five exhibitions to be supported by this program.

The interactive environment of the exhibition was jointly developed by the MIT Media Lab and The Museum of Modern Art and generously supported by Max Palevsky.

Generous support for the installation design is provided by Furniture Co.

This publication is made possible by Elise Jaffe and Jeffrey Brown.

The symposium is made possible by Philips Electronics.

Additional funding is provided by an anonymous donor, NEC Technologies, the Norman and Rosita Winston Foundation, The Contemporary Arts Council of The Museum of Modern Art, and Nearlife, Inc.

Produced by the Department of Publications
The Museum of Modern Art, New York
Edited by Laura Morris
Designed by Antony Drobinski, Emsworth Design, Inc.
Production by Christopher Zichello
Set in Nofret and Ocean Sans
Printed on Gleneagle Dull by Meridian Printing, East Greenwich, Rhode Island
Bound by Mueller Trade Bindery Corp., Middletown, Connecticut

Library of Congress Catalogue Card Number: 99-074231
ISBN: 0-87070-097-9 (MoMA, T&H)
ISBN: 0-8109-6199-7 (Abrams)

Published by The Museum of Modern Art, 11 West 53 Street, New York, New York 10019. www.moma.org

Distributed in the United States and Canada by Harry N. Abrams, Inc., New York. www.abramsbooks.com
Distributed outside the United States and Canada by Thames & Hudson, Ltd., London

Printed in the United States of America

Cover: Rem Koolhaas, Office for Metropolitan Architecture. Maison à Bordeaux, France. 1998

Frontispiece: Shigeru Ban. Curtain Wall House, Tokyo. 1995

Contents

6   Foreword   GLENN D. LOWRY

7   Preface and Acknowledgments   TERENCE RILEY

9   The Un-Private House   TERENCE RILEY

39   Projects

40   WINKA DUBBELDAM, ARCHI-TECTONICS   Millbrook Residence

44   FRANK LUPO/DANIEL ROWEN, ARCHITECTS   Lipschutz/Jones Apartment

48   HERZOG & DE MEURON   Kramlich Residence and Media Collection

52   DILLER + SCOFIDIO   Slow House

56   HARIRI & HARIRI   The Digital House

60   MVRDV   Two Houses on Borneo Sporenburg

64   MICHAEL BELL   Glass House @ 2°

68   BERNARD TSCHUMI   The Hague Villa

72   SHIGERU BAN   Curtain Wall House

76   MICHAEL MALTZAN ARCHITECTURE   Hergott Shepard Residence

80   FRANCOIS DE MENIL, ARCHITECT   Shorthand House

84   SCOGIN ELAM AND BRAY ARCHITECTS   64 Wakefield

88   FARJADI FARJADI ARCHITECTS   BV House

92   REM KOOLHAAS, OFFICE FOR METROPOLITAN ARCHITECTURE   Maison à Bordeaux

96   XAVEER DE GEYTER ARCHITECTENBUREAU   House in Brasschaat

100   JOEL SANDERS, ARCHITECT   House for a Bachelor

104   PRESTON SCOTT COHEN   Torus House

108   SIMON UNGERS WITH THOMAS KINSLOW   T-House

112   THOMAS HANRAHAN AND VICTORIA MEYERS, ARCHITECTS   Holley Loft

116   KOLATAN/MAC DONALD STUDIO   Ost/Kuttner Apartment

120   CLORINDO TESTA, ARCHITECT   Ghirardo-Kohen House

124   SANAA/KAZUYO SEJIMA, RYUE NISHIZAWA & ASSOCIATES   M House

128   UN STUDIO/VAN BERKEL & BOS   Möbius House

132   GUTHRIE + BURESH ARCHITECTS   WorkHouse

136   NEIL M. DENARI   Massey House

140   STEVEN HOLL ARCHITECTS   Y House

145   Project Information

150   Credits

Foreword

In 1932, The Museum of Modern Art staged its first exhibition of architecture, which would become known as the "International Style" show. *Modern Architecture: International Exhibition* was curated by Henry-Russell Hitchcock and Philip Johnson and enthusiastically endorsed by Alfred H. Barr, Jr., the Museum's founding director. Midway through the exhibition's development, in May 1931, Johnson wrote to one of the participating architects: "For the public, it is my opinion that the most interesting exhibit is still that of the private house, and I wish to have as many private houses as I can."

Johnson's belief that the public would be most interested in private houses was based on two premises. First, the nonprofessional might be better able to understand a house than more complex building types. Secondly, and more importantly, was his recognition of the place that the house plays in the public imagination. As the philosopher Gaston Bachelard said in *The Poetics of Space,* "Our house. . . . is our first universe, a real cosmos in every sense of the word." Johnson also understood that the private house as a building type served as an experimental laboratory for architecture, particularly among his contemporaries. The landmark 1932 exhibition would feature four buildings that quickly came to be seen as architectural

masterpieces, all of them private houses: Le Corbusier's Villa Savoye, Ludwig Mies van der Rohe's Tugendhat House, J. J. P. Oud's House in Pinehurst, North Carolina, and Frank Lloyd Wright's project for a House on the Mesa.

Like these buildings, the twenty-six projects assembled in *The Un-Private House* by Terence Riley, Chief Curator, Department of Architecture and Design, represent transformations of the cultural invention of the house in light of contemporary influences. Some of these are societal, such as changing family composition and increased numbers of people working at home. Other influences relate more to significant shifts within the discipline of architecture. New technologies have opened up new avenues of exploration, from complex geometries to interactive environments.

Perhaps the most startling thing to realize about so many of these houses is that, despite some of their formal complexities, one can recognize in them the echo of the work of Mies van der Rohe. If the decline of his influence upon architects in recent decades was in large part Oedipal, his renewed importance is distinctly millennial. One hundred years ago, the advent of the twentieth century was a topic of great interest and eagerly anticipated. The twentieth century is still the

focus of great interest, and few look to the next with the same unalloyed excitement as their predecessors. At this moment, when the future that was once so eagerly awaited is going to become, at least numerically, the undisputed past, it is evident that, just as the quattrocento became the point of reference for the cinquecento, the tides that coursed through the twentieth century will flow into the next as well.

The Un-Private House is the first of five exhibitions to be supported over the next ten years by the new Lily Auchincloss Fund for Contemporary Architecture, which is named in honor of Lily Auchincloss, Trustee of The Museum of Modern Art from 1971 to 1996 and Chairman of the Museum's Committee on Architecture and Design from 1981 to 1995. I am most grateful to Terry Riley for having conceived this exhibition series and for bringing his insight and scholarship to the task of studying this most important building form. Like many landmark exhibitions undertaken by The Museum of Modern Art, *The Un-Private House* is as provocative as it is engaging, reflecting the Museum's commitment to the exploration of critical issues in contemporary architecture.

GLENN D. LOWRY
Director, The Museum of Modern Art, New York

Preface and Acknowledgments

Spending a lot of time, as I do, looking at architecture, I realized nearly two years ago that a great deal of the interesting work that I was seeing consisted of private houses. Over the course of the last year and a half, the research and development of this project have proved my early musings about the private house—its past and, more importantly, its present and future—to be an exhibition and book well worth pursuing. As both an indicator of architecture's direction and a reflection of culture, the house holds a special fascination.

I would like to thank the architects for their many contributions to this exhibition and publication: their talents and their thoughts, not to mention the drawings, models, photographs, and other materials they have lent. I would also like to record my indebtedness to their clients; if it were not for their spirited vision, the architects would not have had the opportunity to achieve such extraordinary designs.

I also thank Glenn D. Lowry, Director, and all the senior staff members of The Museum of Modern Art, for their dedicated support of this project in all of its complexity—in spite of its apparent ability to expand spontaneously. In addition, I am grateful to a number of individuals, both in- and outside the Museum, who spent time discussing the idea with me, provided resources, or otherwise offered encouragement: John Elderfield, Chief Curator at Large; Beatrice Kernan, Assistant Deputy Director for Curatorial Affairs; John Bennett; Barry Bergdoll; Jeffrey Kipnis; Seamus Moran; Stephen Perrella; and Gwendolyn Wright.

From the Museum's Department of Publications, Laura Morris, Editor, served as a patient and astute critic and adviser in turning my draft text into an exceptional publication. Christopher Zichello, Associate Production Manager, oversaw its production with his customary sense of perfection. Jasmine Moorhead, Assistant Editor, also made important contributions to this book and edited all the exhibition-related texts. Antony Drobinski of Emsworth Design must be recognized for the catalogue's clear and compelling design. Michael Maegraith, Publisher; Harriet Bee, Managing Editor; and Nancy Kranz, Manager, Promotion and Special Services, have also furthered the book's realization.

The exhibition is the better for Andrew Davies, Production Manager, Exhibition Design and Production, who participated in all aspects of its design and planning. David Schaefer of Furniture Co. not only lent the furniture used in the exhibition, much of which he designed, but also made his considerable talents in planning available to us. Anne Anderson, Senior Graphic Designer, designed many components of the exhibition identity, and Catarina Tsang and Patrick Seymour of Tsang Seymour Design designed the exhibition graphics. Eleni Cocordas, Associate Coordinator, Exhibitions, kept an eye on our accounts, ensuring that our aspirations were equal to our means. Monika Dillon, Director of Development, made sure those means were ever increasing. Linda Karsteter-Stubbs, Senior Assistant Registrar, deftly organized and oversaw the complex transport arrangements.

It was particularly rewarding to collaborate with Professor Neil Gershenfeld of the MIT Media Lab and his students in developing the exhibition's interactive component. On the Museum's side, Greg Van Alstyne, Design Manager, New Media; Paul Niebuhr, Director, Information Systems; and Davies made significant contributions to the conceptualization of the multimedia environment's design.

Jessica Ferraro, Publicity Coordinator, has worked diligently to assure that the media have become aware of the project and understand its message, enabling both the exhibition and this catalogue to reach the greatest possible audience. Maribel Bastian, Education Coordinator, translated that message into thoughtful educational programs for the public. The efforts of Anne Davy, Assistant Director, Event Planning and Communications Systems, has guaranteed that all of our visitors will feel welcome at the exhibition.

It is difficult to describe how much work goes into a project of this sort. In my own department, may it suffice to say that without the efforts of Curbie Oestreich, Assistant to the Chief Curator, and Bevin Howard, Research Assistant, *The Un-Private House* would still be an idea in a curator's head. Oestreich, despite numerous other responsibilities, carefully planned diverse aspects of the project, demonstrating a remarkable ability to deliver excellent results. Howard's efforts extended far beyond the usual. Her critical advice and innovative proposals were essential to the project's conception and realization. Inevitably, the other members of the Department of Architecture and Design have been pulled into this undertaking in various ways. I am grateful for the involvement of Paola Antonelli, Curator; Peter Reed, Curator; Matilda McQuaid, Associate Curator; Christopher Mount, Assistant Curator; Abby Pervil, Executive Secretary; Luisa Lorch, Cataloguer; and Pierre Adler, The Lily Auchincloss Study Center for Architecture and Design Supervisor.

In closing, I would like to note my personal regard for the memory of Lily Auchincloss. Her unflagging dedication to the arts of architecture and design continues to sustain our endeavors at the Museum through the generosity of her daughter, Alexandra Herzan.

TERENCE RILEY
Chief Curator, Department of Architecture and Design
The Museum of Modern Art, New York

TERENCE RILEY The Un-Private House

All of architecture is colored by the problem of the house.

JEAN HÉLION[1]

Jean Hélion's words point out the unique position the private house has played throughout the history of architecture. Despite its relatively small size, at least compared to other architectural programs, the house figures large in the cultural imagination. It has been and continues to be the man–made environment's fundamental building block, its most irreducible component, providing an essential daily need: shelter. Even so, its broad appeal cannot be considered a function of necessity alone. Closely identified with the individual and the nuclear family, it has been frequently considered as an expression of widely held, even universal, values. Conversely, the private house has also been emblematic of more subjective desires, desires that change not only from person to person but from generation to generation.

While individual domiciles existed in the world of classical antiquity, the private house as we know it today traces its lineage to seventeenth–century Europe and colonial New England.[2] This new type frequently mimicked the contemporaneous palaces and villas of the upper classes in its architectural style, decoration, and relationship to the landscape. However, the character-istic that had the greatest influence on the private house's development was not architectural fashion but the prerequisite of privacy itself.

Although it is precisely defined in the dictionary—"the quality or state of being apart from company or observation: seclusion"[3]—the term privacy is a thoroughly relative one. It has evolved over centuries and continues to do so. Nonetheless, the privacy in the private house, since its inception, has been predicated on a discernible separation of its inhabitants and activities from both the public realm and other houses. The private house has also been from its establishment a building type that enshrines family life to the exclusion of all other activities. Furthermore, as a space so dedicated, it has been for almost four hundred years largely responsible for the creation and develop-ment of those rituals and comforts that we now associate with the domestic.

Taken literally, the term private house might apply to any dwelling that shelters an individual or family, whether it is a palace or a tent. However, in Western culture the private house has been the subject of tremendous interest and controversy in that it has been considered as a type of housing intended for a specific class of people: the bourgeoisie in Europe and the middle class in the United States. As such, the concept of the private house has become asso-ciated with a range of political, moral, social, and economic issues.

This confluence of associations, and their potential volatility, is amply illustrated in Bernard Edelman's *La Maison de Kant*, a reflection on the life and thinking of the Enlightenment philosopher Immanuel Kant: "The house, the residence, is the only rampart against the dread of nothingness, darkness, and the obscurity of the past…. Man's identity is thus residential, and that is why the revolutionary, who has neither hearth nor home, hence neither faith nor law, epitomizes the anguish of errancy…. The man without a home is a potential criminal."[4]

Preston Scott Cohen. Torus House, Old Chatham, New York. Projected completion 2001. Computer-generated image

A contemporary of Kant, Thomas Jefferson, characterized his own house in much different terms, drawing parallels between it and his homeland. From Paris he wrote, "I am savage enough to prefer the woods, the wilds, and the independence of Monticello, to all the brilliant pleasures of this gay Capital. I shall, therefore, rejoin myself to my native country, with new attachments, and with exaggerated esteem for its advantages; for though there is less wealth there, there is more freedom, more ease, and less misery."[5] Despite the divergence in Kant's and Jefferson's respective points of view, their ideas equally portrayed a vision of society, in Europe and in the United States, in which the private house was playing a more and more central role. Furthermore, over the course of the nineteenth century, whatever root differences might have existed between European and American conceptions of the private house were heading toward convergence. That which we now refer to as the "traditional" private house developed on either side of the Atlantic as an expression of individual freedom and, paradoxically, as a commitment to shared societal values.

Throughout the Western world, the private house's popularity has not dimmed during the twentieth century. In Europe, a substantial amount of the housing stock is dedicated to private houses, despite the relatively dense patterns of urbanization.[6] In the United States and Canada, the percentages of private houses are significantly higher—as are the numbers of detached houses—which reflect the sparser settlement patterns in North America. In 1998, seventy-six percent of the approximately 1.7 million new housing units in construction in the United States were private houses.[7] In Canada, detached houses outnumber attached dwellings by more than five to one.[8]

Experience suggests that the great majority of these houses, whether attached or detached, largely conform to the same "traditional" physical characteristics. The typical structure would have a series of common rooms, such as living, dining, and family rooms, and a number of separate bedrooms. The former would be on a lower level, and the latter on an upper level. The design of most of these houses would also undoubtedly have a "traditional" appearance, with peaked roof, shuttered windows, and ornamental details, evoking the domestic culture developed over so many years of Western civilization.

Even so, the current ubiquity of the private house in its most traditional form is rife with contradiction. The social conditions and structures that drove the development of the private house—privacy, the separation of living and work, the family, domesticity—have all changed drastically, perhaps more so in the last fifty years than in the preceding four centuries. In contrast to the self-evident majority, a new and notable generation of house designs—commissioned by forward-thinking clients—is addressing not only critical architectural issues but also the cultural parameters of the private house.

The Presence of the Public

From the early seventeenth century, when the private house began to develop as a broadly popular type, until the 1920s, when the electronic radio was introduced into the home, the privacy in the private house grew as the presence of the public world diminished. The architectural historian Spiro Kostof reminds us just how large this public presence could be in earlier times: "The medieval town house is not only the family home, it is also a

FIGURE 1: *Jew's House, Lincoln, England. c. 1170–80*

FIGURE 2: *Artist unknown.* The Birth of Caterina Cornaro. *c. 1550–1600. Oil on wood, 16 7/16 x 20 9/16" (41.8 x 52.2 cm). Isabella Stewart Gardner Museum, Boston*

FIGURE 3: *Carl Larsson.* Cozy Corner. *1890–97. Watercolor, 12 5/8 x 16 15/16" (32 x 43 cm). Nationalmuseum, Stockholm*

manufacturing locale, counting house, store, or shop."[9] In addition, the so-called big house of the Middle Ages, such as the Jew's House in Lincoln, England (fig. 1), sheltered the owner and his family along with relatives, employees, apprentices, servants, and frequent guests. Those guests, perhaps friends or relatives, were just as likely to have been on business with the owner, who, in the absence of hotels and restaurants, would have been expected to provide meals and lodging. The public character of these houses is further underscored by the lack of separate rooms for these various activities. In most instances, the inhabitants lived, slept, and ate in large, open halls that accommodated different functions principally by the rearrangement of furniture. The realization of privacy within the house was an evolutionary process that unfolded over centuries. During the Renaissance and on into later eras, bourgeois and even aristocratic families continued to inhabit medieval-style halls. This way of living is suggested by a painting from the sixteenth century, *The Birth of Caterina Cornaro* (fig. 2), in which a great number of people are milling about, talking, and preparing food, while attendants aid a new mother who lies in bed at the left of the panel.

Nonetheless, beginning in the seventeenth century, the rising economic fortunes of the bourgeoisie were inversely reflected in the declining presence of the public in the home. By the early nineteenth century, the distinction between the private house and the public world had become so refined that it was thought to reflect various broader dualities as well, among them suburb and city, craft and industry, and nature and artifice. The literary critic Walter Benjamin came to see the nineteenth-century private house as not only separate from the public world but, more significantly, as a retreat from it. In his essay "Louis-Philippe, or the Interior," he wrote, "For the private person, living space becomes, for the first time, antithetical to the place of work."[10] The art historian Michelle Facos has applied Benjamin's position to Lilla Hyttnäs, the family home of the Swedish artist Carl Larsson. Larsson documented the interiors of the house in a series of watercolors published in 1899 as *A Home*. Coupled with Larsson's own words, an example of the illustrations, *Cozy Corner* (fig. 3), epitomizes the transformed role of the private house: "Here I experienced that unspeakably sweet feeling of seclusion from the noise of the world."[11]

Even as the middle classes in America and Europe strove to limit the intrusion of the public into their increasingly private realm, they retained a natural fascination for the outside world as represented by what we would today call the media in its earliest incarnations. The presence of books, maps, and works of art tempered the inward-looking nature of the private house. In the nineteenth century, a study or library—a room devoted to books, newspapers, magazines, and journals—was not uncommon in an upper-middle-class home.

Today, the private house has become a permeable structure, receiving and transmitting images, sounds, text, and data. The German philosopher Martin Heidegger made particular note of the fundamental difference between the presence of the newer, electronic media and the more traditional media, which had been present in the house over the centuries. In his essay "The Thing," Heidegger expressed concern over the way in which the electronic broadcasting of words and images alters our fundamental relationship, that is, our distance, from events and things: "What is this uniformity in

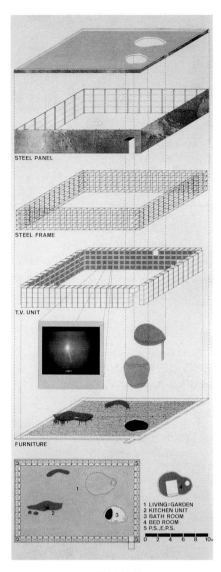

FIGURE 4: *Takahide Nozawa,
TV Garden. Another Glass House
competition proposal, 1991*

which everything is neither far nor near—is, as it were, without distance? Everything gets lumped together into uniform distancelessness. How? Is not this merging of everything into the distanceless more unearthly than everything bursting apart?"[12]

What Heidegger called distancelessness has been instrumental in the profound transformation of, among other things, the relationship between the private house and the media in the second half of the twentieth century. The extent of this transformation might be evident in comparing Larsson's Lilla Hyttnäs, where he found that "sweet feeling of seclusion," and Takahide Nozawa's 1991 design for a house entitled TV Garden (fig. 4). Taking its floor plan from Ryoan-ji, the walled rock garden in Kyoto that has become an international icon of contemplation and serenity, TV Garden is essentially a graveled living space that is enclosed on all four sides by 245 television screens mounted in a steel frame. "Rocks" interspersed in the graveled area contain bathroom, bedroom, and kitchen. The then twenty-five-year-old architect explained that the relationship between the inhabitants of the house and the media would equal that found "among natural elements in the garden."[13]

Nozawa's inference of a "natural" relationship between the media and the inhabitants of a house is wholly outside of Heidegger's conception of "being," in German, *Dasein*. In his text *Being and Time*, the philosopher questioned the effect of the media on daily life: "All the ways in which we speed things up, as we are more or less compelled to do today, push us on towards the conquest of remoteness. With the 'radio', for example, Dasein has so expanded its everyday environment that it has accomplished a de-severance of the 'world'—a de-severance which, in its meaning for Dasein, cannot yet be visualized."[14]

At the end of the twentieth century, the new kind of relationship to the world of events and things that Heidegger could not visualize, a new kind of distance in daily life with its own parameters and definitions, is clearly evident in the ascendancy of digital technologies throughout everyday life. In both theory and practice, the media's potential effect on space has become a catalyst for contemporary architectural innovation and experimentation. While it is more and more common to find a "media room" in newer houses, such as the unbuilt Millbrook Residence (pp. 40–43) by Winka Dubbeldam of Archi-Tectonics for a site in New York State, more profound innovations are also evident. In Frank Lupo's and Daniel Rowen's Lipschutz/Jones Apartment (pp. 44–47) in New York City, digital screens displaying financial information are visible throughout the loft, alerting the owners to fluctuations in international currency markets. In Jacques Herzog's and Pierre de Meuron's Kramlich Residence and Media Collection (pp. 48–51), to be built in Napa Valley, California, the interior partitions of the house are screens onto which the owners' collection of video art is projected. These architectural manifestations of electronic events do, indeed, represent the distancelessness that Heidegger believed was a threat to the dwelling. But this distancelessness has become a commonplace, and Heidegger's unease has been replaced by an equally common awareness of the distinction between the real and the virtual.

Elizabeth Diller's and Ricardo Scofidio's Slow House (pp. 52–55), an unbuilt weekend house designed for a site on Long Island, New York, provides an example of the architects' implicit recognition of the duality of the real and the virtual, emphasizing in particular their relationship to consumption and possession. The rear of the house, which faces the desirable view, is opened up by means of a picture window that frames the landscape beyond. A video camera mounted above the house captures the same landscape digitally and transmits it back to a monitor suspended before the picture window, as if to compete electronically with, or even perfect, the "actual" view. In the architects' words, "The view may be recorded and deferred… day played back at night, fair weather played back in foul. The view is also portable; it can be transmitted to different locations in the house or back to the primary residence in the city."[15] How and what one views becomes completely subjective.

In a more speculative manner, other architects are trying to envisage how the "virtual house" might be realized and how it might reflect the more prosaic needs of daily life. The Digital House project (pp. 56–59), designed by Gisue Hariri and Mojgan Hariri for *House Beautiful* magazine, and Hyper House Pavilion 5 (fig. 5), a project by Michael Trudgeon and Anthony Kitchener, are examples of such an effort. Both demonstrate the point made by the architectural critic Beatriz Colomina in assessing the interrelationships between the house and the media: "The way the house occupies the media is directly related to the way the media occupies the house."[16]

While the interior surfaces of Herzog's and de Meuron's Kramlich Residence are meant to serve as screens onto which digital art is projected, both the interior and exterior surfaces of Trudgeon's and Kitchener's Hyper House Pavilion 5 and Hariri's and Hariri's Digital House are conceived as "smart skins" that blur the distinction between the computer and architecture and perform various functions to assist or enhance daily living. In The Digital House project, a Julia Child–like character pops up over the kitchen counter to provide advice on food preparation, and digital guests appear in the living room for a virtual visit. From every vantage point, the house has the ability to receive and transmit information, illustrating what media theorist Neil Gershenfeld has called "mature technologies" in which it is "not possible to isolate the form and the function."[17] The Hyper House is equally permeable. According to one of its designers, "The mullions support the glass skin, which has fully adjustable optical and thermal properties. At the south end, a television image is being directly displayed from the glass skin. Also a message to the neighbors has been programmed onto the electrochromic layer of the glass skin."[18]

Just as architects are imagining what might be called the "un-private house," so are others imagining its inhabitants. The cultural historian Donna Haraway offers the following in "A Manifesto for Cyborgs": "The cyborg is resolutely committed to partiality, irony, intimacy, and perversity. It is oppositional, utopian, and completely without innocence. No longer structured by the polarity of public and private, the cyborg defines a technological polis based partly on a revolution of social relations in the *oikos*, the household. Nature and culture are reworked; the one can no longer be the resource for appropriation or incorporation by the other."[19]

PRIVACY

The implications of Haraway's manifesto for everyday life are difficult to grasp, much less idealize. Readers who are both familiar with and disturbed by the image of the cyborg (that is, cybernetic organism) may recognize the chasm between Haraway's vision of a postmodern cyber–culture and the world of the Enlightenment evoked in Edelman's *La Maison de Kant*. Moreover,

FIGURE 5: *Michael Trudgeon, Crowd Productions P/L, and Anthony Kitchener, Cash Engineering Research P/L. Hyper House Pavilion 5, St. Andrews Beach, Victoria, Australia. Unbuilt, 1998. Computer-generated image by Glynis Teo*

they might recognize how recently and how quickly that gap has made itself manifest in contemporary society. Even a generation ago, the philosopher Hannah Arendt could cite the modern concepts of nation and society as reconfigurations of the *oikos* and polis of ancient Greece and Rome, albeit on a scale far beyond that of the city-state from which they emerged. Although Arendt saw these reconfigurations as having effectively "blurred" the idea of private and public, they were still dependent on the concept of the household and public realms as "distinct, separate entities."[20] Haraway's "technological polis" can be seen not only as a successor to the modern nation as defined by Arendt but also as a new political realm, one in which the duality of public and private is no longer an operative concept. In her discussion of the dynamics between public and private life in the classical period, Arendt also pointed out that Zeus Herkeios, the protector of borderlines, safeguarded these distinctions in the minds of the ancient Greeks.[21] In a piece written for the *New Yorker* recently, Nancy Franklin seems to have been hoping that the ancient god still existed: "The national pastime, playable in all four seasons, has become show-and-tell, and there are few among us who don't occasionally want to avert our eyes, or close them, in the hope of rediscovering, at least in our own minds, the line between private life and public exposure."[22]

Before looking at how the increased fluidity in the concept of privacy has influenced contemporary design, it is useful to consider again how refined the notion of privacy in the private house had become by the twentieth century. For this purpose, Frank Lloyd Wright's A Home in a Prairie Town (fig. 6), an idealized house design, can be considered as a highly articulated vision of domestic architecture. Wright's project was commissioned by and first published in the progressive *Ladies' Home Journal*. The project was comprised of not only the design for the house but also a "block plan" for four identical houses, affording each "absolute privacy" with respect to the public and the other three.[23] The extent to which Wright strove to achieve that "absolute privacy" is notable. His model house is set back from the property line, with a low wall and planting marking a threshold between the public circulation of the street and the approach to the house. The entrance to the house is recessed within the body of the house and shielded by low eaves. The window openings facing the street are relatively small and are located high up, under the eaves; the inhabitants could see out to the natural world, but the public could not peer in. The library, which flanks the walk leading to the front door, has no windows facing the walk, preventing visitors from glimpsing the inhabitants within.

While the intimacy and coziness promised by such a house might be seen as an end in itself, Wright's words confirm that his emphasis on privacy in the private house was also related to political considerations: "America.... places a life premium upon individuality,—the highest possible development of the individual consistent with a harmonious whole.... It means lives lived in greater independence and seclusion."[24]

The politics of privacy have been ever volatile but are now being further roiled by the increased presence of the electronic media in people's homes and daily lives. Writing recently, with considerable alarm, on the proliferation of electronic media, the *New York Times* columnist William Safire said: "Your right to privacy has been stripped away. You cannot walk into your bank, or apply for a job, or access your personal computer, without undergoing the

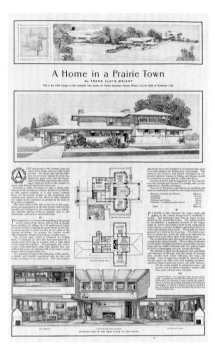

FIGURE 6: *Frank Lloyd Wright.
A Home in a Prairie Town. Project, 1900.
Page from* Ladies' Home Journal,
February 1901

FIGURE 7: *Ludwig Mies van der Rohe. Farnsworth House, Plano, Illinois. 1946–51*

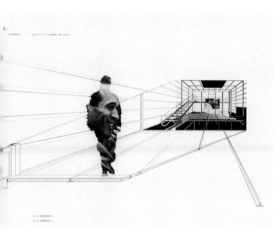

FIGURE 8: *Gordon Kipping, G-TECTS. "3.9.00000000 Entity As Information Zoom." 1995. From* Ordinary Diagrams, *2nd ed. (Los Angeles: Public Access Press at the Southern California Institute of Architecture, 1997), sec. 3.9.*

scrutiny of strangers…. Big Brother is watching as never before…. Isn't it time to reverse that terrible trend toward national nakedness before it replaces privacy as an American value?"[25] Safire's invocation of the draconian image of Big Brother interjects the alarming predictions made by George Orwell in his novel of fifty years ago, *1984*, for a faceless society with a diminished sense of individualism and privacy. Underlying Safire's position is his exasperation with a public that seems increasingly unmoved by Orwell's concerns.

In architectural terms, The Digital House, which is designed to maximize the same technologies that arouse Safire's suspicions, is potentially more Orwellian than anything Orwell could have imagined. Even Gershenfeld cautions, "We should now worry less about control *of* the means of communication and more about control *by* the means of communication."[26] Yet to the broad public, this image apparently fails to universally incite the same anxieties. Furthermore, The Digital House obviously meets the approval of *House Beautiful* magazine, which a generation ago fumed about the International Style and Bauhaus design. In her 1953 article "The Threat to the Next America," Elizabeth Gordon wrote: "For if we can be sold on accepting dictators in matters of taste and how our homes are to be ordered, our minds are certainly well prepared to accept dictators in other departments of life."[27] In this context, she derisively referred to Ludwig Mies van der Rohe's Farnsworth House (fig. 7) as "a one-room house that is nothing but a glass cage on stilts."[28]

In its *virtual* transparency, The Digital House multiplies the dangers that Gordon saw in the Farnsworth House's *literal* transparency: it did not sufficiently guarantee the privacy of the home; it could not be shielded from the public gaze. Edith Farnsworth herself was, ultimately, no fan of the house, and her words, interweaving literal and technological transparency, reflect it: "The house is transparent, like an X-ray."[29] By contrast, Gordon Kipping's recent project for a "domestic enclosure" (fig. 8) proposes the same kind of conditions in a neutral, if not positive, manner. Using both neologisms and typographic devices to create an aura of technological rationalism, Kipping writes that in his project "the living room facilitates a convergence of transmission and reception through a reordering of surveillance [subject to *Unidirectional Extraction* <3.0.00000011.>]."[30]

Unlike Heidegger, who was concerned about the very presence of the media, Elizabeth Gordon, Orwell, and Safire were concerned about surveillance. Whether the issue is technological or literal transparency, the result is a "nakedness" that, in Safire's opinion, is the antipode to privacy. While Hariri and Hariri, Kipping, and others might find the idea of a "domestic enclosure" that is both a receiver and a transmitter of information to be intellectually appealing, for Safire this concept would undoubtedly call to mind Orwell's "telescreen." That "interactive" device not only brought information into every household in Orwell's fictional Oceania but also provided Big Brother with the ability to view all its inhabitants.

MVRDV's two row houses in the Borneo Sporenburg housing district (on plots twelve and eighteen) in Amsterdam (pp. 60–63) demonstrate that changes in the idea of privacy are not simply matters for theoretical discussion or futuristic projects. As opposed to the Farnsworth House, which was, after all, set in an isolated location, these two row houses, like Michael Bell's Glass House @ 2° design for a site in Houston (pp. 64–67), are located in a fairly dense urban area. Displaying none of Safire's anxiety, MVRDV architect

FIGURE 9: *Bjarne Mastenbroek and MVRDV. Double House, Utrecht, The Netherlands. 1995–97*

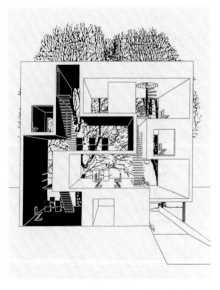

FIGURE 10: *Bjarne Mastenbroek and MVRDV. Double House, Utrecht, The Netherlands. 1995–97. Section*

Winy Maas has said: "Putting the inside, even your own, on display seems a very modern topic. It might be perverse but it has similarities with the mixture of privacy and publicness these days: walking on the zebra crossing [crosswalk] and listening to the love conversation of the neighbour who is phoning his girlfriend, the way people show their privacy on the television in order to attract attention. In such a condition the ancient limitations between privacy and publicity seem to be irrelevant."[31]

In the most common type of private house in Europe, the row house, those "ancient limitations between privacy and publicity" have traditionally been created by the party wall. In the house on plot twelve in Amsterdam, as well as Bjarne Mastenbroek's and MVRDV's Double House (figs. 9, 10), the architects intentionally manipulated that boundary. In the former, despite the narrowness of the site, a semipublic open area was inserted along the party wall, revealing the interior of the house along its glazed length. In the Double House, the architects warped the party wall into a zigzag between the two units. This structure affects in the residents a palpable awareness of their neighbors and the interlocked spaces of the building they share, which clearly counters the logic of the traditional party wall and the privacy it affords.

Bernard Tschumi has displayed a similar nonchalance about the literal and virtual permeability of his unbuilt Hague Villa (pp. 68–71).[32] Referring to its transparent parts' orientation toward the public boundary of the site, the architect remarked: "The house is to be seen as an extension of city events and a momentary pause in the digital transfer of information. The borders of the living room and work space, devoid of the camouflage of ornament, expand beyond the property lines just as they [the property lines] are undermined by the electronic devices of everyday use."[33] Another example of a transparent house within a dense urban landscape is Shigeru Ban's Curtain Wall House (pp. 72–75) in Tokyo, which erodes the border between public and private in a notable and even startling way. The outer skin of the house is comprised of two elements: transparent glass panels and fabric curtains the size of boating sails. Both glass and fabric can be drawn back to open up the interior to the surrounding neighborhood. The result is a "nakedness" that even those who live in glass houses might find surprising.

In Taeg Nishimoto's Plot House (No. 1) project (fig. 11), the "nakedness" of the house involves virtual and actual transparencies between the public and private worlds and also transparencies within the house itself. Nishimoto has used the form of a fragmented conversation, which the reader seemingly overhears, to describe an environment that intermingles the idea of scrutiny from outside with that from within:

6. When I see the shadow of her robe hanging on the bedroom sliding door, I know she is sleeping.

7. The bed takes up the whole room.

8. "Bob, don't you think it's kind of embarrassing leaving the box of condoms on the glass shelf?" "Our bedroom walls are filled with all sorts of junk, nobody will even notice."[34]

This idea of surveillance is taken to its natural conclusion in Kipping's domestic enclosure, wherein technology allows individuals to observe themselves. Unlike a conventional bathroom mirror, the project's "electronic mirror consists of four surveillance cameras each positioned at a quadrant in relation to the position for self-surveillance."[35]

It is, perhaps, tempting to interpret these contemporary attitudes as simple narcissism, through which daily life becomes an endless reflex between voyeurism and exhibitionism. Yet it is possible to see a more critical position within these new attitudes. Wright's interwoven concepts of privacy and individualism are expressed in his prescription for "lives lived in greater independence and seclusion." Could it be that at the end of the twentieth century the splendid isolation envisioned by Wright simply no longer suggests the sense of well-being it once did? Or has this isolation now become associated with alienation as much as independence?

Consider the project of Alex van Es, a systems analyst from the town of Apeldoorn in The Netherlands, who has linked his doorbell, refrigerator, toilet, alarm clock, and six cameras within his house to the Internet. (Is it possible that the Dutch, having practically invented the notion of domestic privacy, are now the least compelled by it?) Van Es allows a public viewing of various intimate details of his life, as well as tabulations of the number of times he went to the refrigerator, what he ate, how many times he went to the toilet, how many visitors he had, and so on. Visitors to his Web site can even determine which music will play to wake him in the morning.[36]

Van Es's project reminds us that the root of the word regard, meaning to look or gaze at, comes from the Old French *garder*, that is, to guard or watch over. Through van Es's invitation to the public to observe the more intimate aspects of his domestic routines, it is possible to recognize that someone watching is not necessarily threatening. Rather, his position suggests that, in a world of isolation, having someone watching can be reassuring. While it remains problematic to reconcile such an attitude with the specter of Big Brother, the interactive gaze of the media has now come to represent a comforting presence as much as an intrusive surveillance.

The Family

Radical changes in the concept of privacy are paralleled both in terms of scope and pace by the transformation of the family and family life since World War II. Before considering these changes, it is useful to look at the status quo ante. In the latter half of the nineteenth century, Leo Tolstoy, in the opening lines of his novel *Anna Karenina* (1873–77), wrote, "All happy families are like one another."[37] Despite this overly generalizing tone, Tolstoy's words

FIGURE 11: *Taeg Nishimoto. Plot House (No. 1). Project, 1992. Elevation*

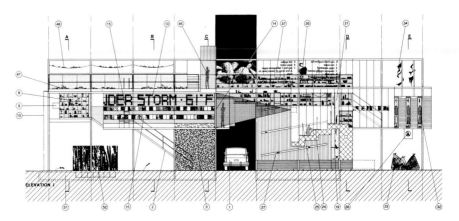

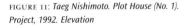

have the ring of truth. Perhaps the reason Tolstoy could say that all happy families were alike was that society wished them to be so. By the nineteenth century, the term family referred more and more to the nuclear family— father-husband, mother-wife, and children—and less and less to the idea of the family as an extended group of people related by blood, marriage, and other circumstances. Another idealized observation, this one from earlier in the nineteenth century, speaks about the private house as nearly inseparable from the family: "The possession of an entire house is strongly desired by every Englishman; for it throws a sharp well-defined circle round his family and hearth—the shrine of his sorrows, joys and meditations."[38] This relationship between the bourgeois or middle-class family and the private house acquired a strong political dimension, as we have seen, since it represented individual liberties. At the same time, ironically, the private house also came to be seen as a means of enforcing social order and as a symbol of moral values. The historian Catherine Hall notes that the nineteenth-century English "Evangelicals saw the family as central to their struggle to reform manners and morals. Families could be the 'little church' which the Puritans had dreamt of, the 'little state' subject to its master."[39] The Evangelicals' belief that social order could be best maintained if the head of each family, the parents and particularly the father, enforced moral accountability and raised the children within certain societal boundaries is not unique in history. The attitude that the house should be an incubator for the proper raising of children is, in fact, central to its very inception. In his elegantly written history of the house, urbanist Witold Rybczynski writes, referring to the seventeenth century: "The emergence of the family home reflected the growing importance of the family in Dutch society. The glue that cemented this unit was the presence of children."[40]

In a more recent article that assesses the influence of many twentieth-century avant-garde houses, Rybczynski seems to be restating his observation about the role of children in the development of the private house. He remarks that Robert Venturi's Vanna Venturi House (Chestnut Hill, Pennsylvania, 1959–64) and Philip Johnson's Glass House (New Canaan, Connecticut, 1949) "have not necessarily influenced domestic models for the general public," as they were designed to be "inhabited by only one or two people."[41] While Rybczynski's remarks might be correct historically, it is important to note that today people who live alone or with one other person *are* the general public in many parts of the industrialized world. For example, around a quarter of American households now consist of one person.[42] Half of the families in America consist of couples without any children living under the same roof.[43] These statistics cannot be considered simply an indication of the aging of the population. The great increase in the number of women with professional careers, experience tells us, has created a proportionate increase in the number of younger couples, well into their thirties, without children. While many of these couples will have children eventually, they will have fewer than a generation ago, and, hence, will spend fewer years of their adult lives raising children. As such, it appears safe to say that a majority of Americans will spend a large part of their lives living alone or with a partner, but not necessarily with children.

This new phenomenon is mirrored in a *New York Times* article by Joseph Giovannini about a childless couple's search for a home: "Instead of a typical

Third level

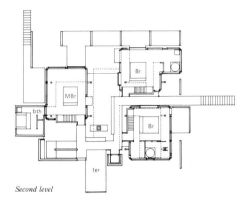

Second level

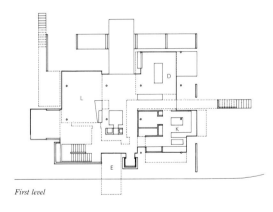

First level

FIGURE 12: *José Oubrerie and Cicely Wylde-Oubrerie, Atelier Wylde-Oubrerie. Miller House, Lexington, Kentucky. 1992. Third-, second-, and ground-floor plans showing three separate "houses" on top levels, and shared spaces on ground level*

high-end house, what they really wanted was a New York loft, set in Santa Barbara."[44] Realizing that the design of most suburban houses reflected the requirements and living patterns of a family with children, they decided to hire an architect to design a home that would fit their own needs. The newspaper article points out, among other things, the very different spatial requirements a couple with children has compared to those of a couple (or, by inference, a single person) without children. Without the need for acoustic and visual privacy, as one would have with children in the house, the traditional upstairs/downstairs separation of the private and public spaces is less compelling. Instead, the loft model has been deemed to be appropriate; its flexibility and openness are in marked contrast to the structured spaces that typify the traditional family house and reflect domestic rituals revolving around the presence of children. While none of them are literally lofts, Dubbeldam's Millbrook Residence and Lupo's and Rowen's Lipschutz/Jones Apartment, both designed for young couples without children; Michael Maltzan's Hergott Shepard Residence (pp. 76–79) in Beverly Hills, built for a gay couple; and Francois de Menil's Shorthand House (pp. 80–83) in Houston, built for a divorced woman whose children are now adults, are all good demonstrations of that spatial option.[45]

The possibilities of the loftlike space are also expressed in Mack Scogin's and Merrill Elam's 64 Wakefield (pp. 84–87) in Atlanta. Scogin and Elam chose to drastically reconfigure their already much renovated bungalow, eliminating many of the partitions between rooms and, perhaps most notably, installing on the upper floor of the house a lap pool, which faces the street but is shielded by a sheet of frosted glass. A critic described the results: "The overlapping spaces are not conceived as a series of planned rooms as much as a choreography of movement. 'I told my mother there are no rooms, just situations,' reports Scogin of the first parental visit. This deliberate ambiguity and open-endedness of 'rooms' is increased by the reflections of the open-air pool against its shimmering glass partial-height walls."[46]

64 Wakefield as well as Homa Farjadi's and Sima Farjadi's BV House (pp. 88–91) in Lancashire, England, also demonstrate other relationships between changing family composition and the private house. The families occupying both consist of parents who had previously been married and children from those earlier marriages. In both designs, separate "houses" for the children were constructed adjacent to the main buildings to afford the children, as well as the parents, a certain sense of autonomy beyond the newly constituted family circles.

The idea of generational separation is not necessarily unique to our own times, and it is certainly not unique to families of second marriages. In the Maison à Bordeaux, designed by Rem Koolhaas of the Office for Metropolitan Architecture (pp. 92–95), two distinct routes lead to the parents' and children's areas. Both are on the upper level, but they are separated by an air space open to the sky above and terrace below. In the case of Xaveer de Geyter's House in Brasschaat (pp. 96–99), the architect has specifically referred to the parents' and children's "apartments," each with its own private garden. Conceived as three separate "houses" within one structure, José Oubrerie's and Cicely Wylde-Oubrerie's Miller House (fig. 12) serves as home base for a far-flung family of four. Oubrerie described his clients, a lawyer, his wife, and their two children: "All four live, work, or study in different parts of the country," with the house accommodating "their various and variable stays, in and out of Lexington, alone or together."[47]

Until just after World War II, only eight percent of American households were comprised of one person. The fact that this number had jumped to approximately twenty-five percent by the last decade of the twentieth century does pose questions. While it is difficult to interpret this data, experience tells us that this dramatic change is due to several factors. First, the general population of the United States is older than it was before World War II; the single occupant of de Menil's Shorthand House, for example, is among the one-third of all American women over the age of sixty who live alone.[48] We also know that it is more socially acceptable to live alone, whether by choice or by circumstances, than it was previously. Underlying the mainstream media uproar about Mies van der Rohe's Farnsworth House was an undeniable suspicion of Dr. Farnsworth herself, a single, professional woman in her late forties, a sufficiently rare phenomenon in 1953 to attract notice.[49] Not only was she neither a wife nor a mother at a time when most women her age were both, but the design of the house indicated she had no particular plans to become part of a family.

The roots of this societal discomfort are deep. In parts of the American colonies, "solitary living," that is, living outside of a family structure, was outlawed.[50] In their effort to enforce social discipline, particularly as it related to sexuality, the Puritans insisted that single adults remain at home, theirs or someone else's, until they established their own "little state subject to its master" through marriage.

The belief that marriage and parenthood is the most desirable state for an adult man or woman is still quite evident in society today. Yet the single person who builds a house for him- or herself is certainly becoming more common. Joel Sanders's unbuilt House for a Bachelor for Minneapolis (pp. 100–03) can be considered to be a sort of domestic manifesto for single people, men and women alike. "If the traditional suburban home laid the foundations for the production of the nuclear family, this project, literally built upon the foundations of a preexisting developer home, reconfigures the interior to sponsor new spatial and visual relationships attuned to the domestic lifestyle of the contemporary bachelor,"[51] writes Sanders. His implicit and explicit affirmation of solitary living could equally apply to Preston Scott Cohen's Torus House (pp. 104–07), the T-House by Simon Ungers with Thomas Kinslow (pp. 108–11), or Thomas Hanrahan's and Victoria Meyers's Holley Loft (pp. 112–15), all of which were designed for single occupants living in New York State.

Part of the anxiety—which has not completely disappeared—about unmarried adult men and women was the ambiguity of their social status and by inference their sexuality. It is difficult to separate the legitimation of the house built for a single person from society's somewhat increased tolerance for social and sexual relationships and lifestyles that fall outside the traditional nuclear-family structure. In this respect, it is interesting to compare recent houses with those from earlier in the twentieth century. Consider the man's bedroom in the Piscator Apartment, designed by Marcel Breuer (fig. 13). At a glance, the solitary white room devoid of works of art or books suggests a mixture of monastic simplicity and military discipline. With its overhanging canopy and continuous head- and sideboard, the narrow bed appears designed to restrain its occupant more than anything else. Aside from a few other pieces of spartan furniture, the only other thing to be seen in the room is exercise equipment, which has clear associations with the health and hygiene culture of the heroic modern period but can also be seen in terms of anxiety over male sexuality. The punching bag, in particular, seems to be a provision for the sublimation of male aggression.

By contrast, richly textured surfaces and lush materials characterize Hanrahan's and Meyers's Holley Loft, designed for a single man. The bedroom is neither spare nor cellular, its ample space clearly visible from the principal public spaces through a glass wall. In a slightly more demure but no less suggestive way, a floating sheet of translucent glass screens the equally spacious bathroom from the living area. An unexpected view reveals the bathtub from the bedroom. In Sanders's House for a Bachelor, the space of the bedroom also flows into the bathing area, complete with pool and, like the Piscator Apartment, exercise equipment. However, in this instance, the health and hygiene associations are overridden by the design's more contemporary and more sensualized references to bodybuilding.

Perceptions about solitary living are certainly not the only manifestations of the moral dimension of the private house. For example, Wright's idealized house design employs what were by the end of the nineteenth century the standard practices of separating the public areas downstairs from the sleeping and bathing rooms upstairs and of isolating as much as possible the individual sleeping and bathing rooms from each other. As the historian Roger-Henri Guerrand has pointed out, "In the nineteenth century a heavy veil was thrown over the least manifestation of sexuality.... Once it had been permissible to receive guests in a room with a bed in it, but that time was past."[52] It would be an exaggeration to say that this practice has ended. However, in recent projects, such as Koolhaas's Maison à Bordeaux and Scogin's and Elam's 64 Wakefield, the clear segregation of public and private is no longer evident. In the Maison à Bordeaux, a central open space allows a hydraulic platform to move between the three floors. This arrangement not only gives mobility to the owner, who uses a wheelchair, but also imparts a new fluidity between the public and private floors of the house. 64 Wakefield also breaks the upstairs/downstairs pattern of private and public. The master-bedroom suite is actually arranged vertically with the sleeping space upstairs and the dressing areas downstairs, both of which are visually screened from visitors but without the "heavy veil" described by Guerrand. In Cohen's Torus House, the veil is completely gone; the sleeping space is adjacent and open to the living area.

Such projects as the Millbrook Residence, the Ost/Kuttner Apartment by Sulan Kolatan and William Mac Donald (pp. 116–19) in New York City, and the House for a Bachelor suggest a contemporary shift in attitudes toward the other "forbidden" domestic space, the bathroom, as well. Unlike the spacious bathing areas in the Holley Loft, the Maison à Bordeaux, and many other projects presented here, the bathroom in the typical middle-class private house has been foremost a functional space, usually no larger than needed to accommodate the standard plumbing fixtures: bathtub, sink, and toilet. Furthermore, the ubiquitous use of ceramic tile, often white, for wall and floor surfaces emphasized hygiene over any other environmental or aesthetic quality. In the Millbrook Residence, the spacious bathroom is open

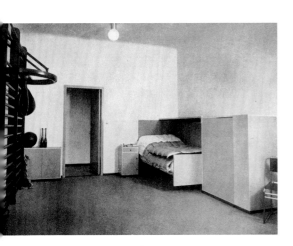

FIGURE 13: *Marcel Breuer.*
Piscator Apartment, Berlin, 1927.
Man's bedroom

to the bedroom, and a wooden soaking tub replaces the standard fixture. From it, the bather can enjoy views into an enclosed court in one direction and out to the landscape in the other. In Kolatan's and Mac Donald's Ost/Kuttner Apartment, the master-bedroom suite is not only fairly open to the public areas but the couple's sleeping and bathing areas are essentially the same space. Only a sheet of transparent glass prevents the water in the bathtub from flowing into the couple's bed. Aside from this transparent membrane, the spaces themselves flow unimpeded one into another, accentuated by the fluid geometries of the cast-fiberglass architectural surfaces. In the House for a Bachelor, the spa replaces the more prosaic bathroom. It is highly visible and also more explicitly eroticized. "An aqueous curtain… veils the backlighted silhouettes of showering bodies," the architect writes.[53]

WORK

By the seventeenth century, the wealth of European town dwellers was such that they were able to physically remove the source generating the family's wealth from the living quarters. Separating the family's business from the house did not just remove the noise but also eliminated the dirt, the employees, the apprentices, the customers, and the suppliers. The house could be, for the first time, quiet, clean, and relatively peaceful. The private house could become a less idiosyncratic and more generic structure; its activities could be more easily defined, and the elements of its design more readily standardized. In effect, it became a building type from which sprang the ubiquitous European row house, the English cottage, and the latter-day American suburban home, among others.

Reversing a process begun nearly four hundred years ago, the reintroduction of work into the private house now under way is extensive, with some twenty million Americans now using their homes as principal workplaces.[54] How working at home affects house design can be seen on a variety of scales. In one instance, a home office might be a fairly contained space that acts as an appendage or an extension of a remote place of work, such as in the Holley Loft. On a larger scale, the home office might be a principal place of work, in which one or more of the occupants spends all of his or her working time, as in Clorindo Testa's Ghirardo-Kohen House (pp. 120–23) in Buenos Aires and Kazuyo Sejima's and Ryue Nishizawa's M House (pp. 124–27) in Tokyo.

In other designs, the presence of work is not limited to a single space, instead merging with the living areas to create a new kind of space, as might be seen in the Lipschutz/Jones Apartment. The owners of this loft are both traders on Wall Street, and, in light of the globalization of international markets, their working hours are no longer fixed. Rather, work occurs when market activity occurs. Hence, the home office is in effect a panopticonlike trading room, its flickering digital screens visible from other areas of the loft. Six screens in addition to those in the office display information at close range in various locations: next to the bathroom mirror (so as to be visible when shaving), next to the bed (to be visible upon waking), and so on.

In a more sculptural way, Ben van Berkel's Möbius House (pp. 128–31) in Het Gooi, The Netherlands, symbolizes the seamless flow of living and working that now characterizes so many lives. The clients are a husband and wife who both work at home. Their separate work areas are folded into the other spaces used in daily life. Unlike the traditional single-family home's

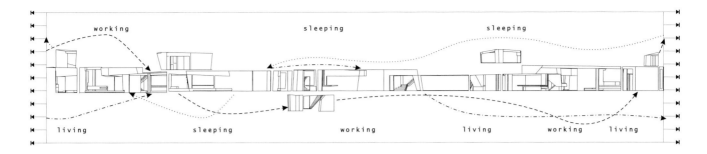

working   sleeping   sleeping

living   sleeping   working   living   working   living

FIGURE 14: *UN Studio/Van Berkel & Bos. Möbius House, Het Gooi, The Netherlands. 1998. Unfolded sections diagramming spatial flow*

sharp functional and social distinctions, the Möbius House's spaces are like intertwined pieces of a ribbon that has no beginning and no end (fig. 14).

Dubbeldam conceived of a similar seamless expression of her clients' daily lives in her design of the Millbrook Residence for a young professional couple. The various work and living functions—as well as the interior and exterior of the house—are woven together like the strands of, in the architect's words, a Celtic knot (fig. 15).[55] The two owners will work on different levels of the house when built. He, a graphic designer, will work on the ground-floor media room, while she will work on fashion-industry projects in a studio on the upper level. While they work separately in their daily routines, the "knotted" structure guarantees that they will constantly crisscross each other as they move through the house.

The BV House by Farjadi and Farjadi is also a place in which the parents work. To both integrate the work space with the parents' quarters and separate it from the social spaces, the Farjadis grouped the parents' and employee's offices with the parents' bedroom, dressing room, and bathing area. A lily pond traversed by bridges separates this "unit" from the main social areas.

In considering a number of these projects, Heidegger's objections to the presence of the media may come to mind. The image of a "seamless" back and forth between living and working no doubt carries with it some anxiety, particularly as it might represent, in a hyper-capitalist world, a life of endless work. Yet, for many, it also carries the somewhat romantic notion of the reintegration of the dualities that have characterized the private house since the nineteenth century: public and private, masculine and feminine, action and repose.

None of these potential reintegrations would be possible without the radical changes wrought by the digital revolution. That these changes have become relatively commonplace can be seen in the example of the graphic designer mentioned above. For the majority of his professional activities, he uses computer equipment, which is connected to his remote clients by modem. Roughly fifteen years after the word processor became an innovation in the workplace, digital technologies have helped reintroduce work into the house, sometimes interweaving it throughout the entire environment, even, as in the Lipschutz/Jones Apartment, on an around-the-clock basis. Furthermore, the result is not some sort of mercantile bedlam breaking out in the living room but the silent flicker of an aestheticized flow of information.

It should be noted that throughout the nineteenth and twentieth centuries the idea of working at home did not completely disappear. For lawyers, doctors, and other professionals in the nineteenth century, an office within the body of the house or even, as in France, within the apartment

FIGURE 15: *An example of Celtic knotwork*

was not uncommon. Pierre Chareau's Maison de Verre (Paris, 1932), comprised of a gynecologist's offices and his home, is a good example of this residential type integrating work and living spaces. The "house of the artist," with roots in the nineteenth-century Arts and Crafts movement, is another type that survived the segregation of the two activities. Reconfigured here in the Torus House, this hybrid combines living space with the artist's studio.

Danelle Guthrie's and Tom Buresh's WorkHouse (pp. 132–35) in Los Angeles, Neil M. Denari's unbuilt Massey House design also for Los Angeles (pp. 136–39), and Reinhold Martin's and Kadambari Baxi's Homeoffice project (1996) merge elements of both the residence/office and the artist's house. Designed as the architects' own residence, the WorkHouse serves as one of many examples of the revitalization of the residence/office model. In the WorkHouse, the boundary between public–work and private–living, which was maintained in the Maison de Verre and the Massey House, is blurred by the single stair that crisscrosses between the two areas, making the building more like the artist's house. The Homeoffice equally blurs the distinctions by reprogramming an existing corporate office tower through interjecting domestic spaces into the existing work spaces.

The WorkHouse, Massey House, and Homeoffice are not the only examples of contemporary houses that subsume additional functions. Larger houses, or at least those whose overall space exceeds the more prosaic requirements of the household, have throughout history included various nondomestic programs under the same roof as more traditional living areas. Koolhaas's Maison à Bordeaux, Maltzan's Hergott Shepard Residence, and Testa's Ghirardo–Kohen House all have ample space dedicated to the exhibition of art, and Unger's and Kinslow's T–House similarly devotes space to its library and reading room. These familiar domestications of often more public programs have been adapted to reflect contemporary concerns in the Kramlich Residence's video galleries and the Millbrook Residence's media room. Spaces related to health and exercise do not have quite as long a tradition as libraries and art galleries. Even so, twentieth-century projects such as Breuer's Piscator Apartment, with its built-in exercise equipment, and Le Corbusier's Unité d'Habitation (Marseilles, 1946–52), with its rooftop running track and pool, established precedents for the workout rooms and swimming pools in the Hergott Shepard Residence, the House for a Bachelor, the Massey House, 64 Wakefield, and various other buildings.

Also notable is the relative proportion of some of these programmatic additions. In the T–House, the volume of space given over to the books is as large as the living quarters, and in the Kramlich Residence it is difficult to say where the living quarters and the video exhibition spaces begin and end. The Torus House is similarly composed. Depending on how the owner chooses to use the space, from twenty to sixty percent of the house serves as an art studio.

Is the T–House then a house with a library or a library with living quarters? Does the owner of the Torus House sleep in his studio or paint in his house? Do Lipschutz and Jones as well as Guthrie and Buresh work in their homes or live in their offices? In each case, we are reminded that the separation of work and living into separate spaces was the catalyst for the development of the office and the house as distinct architectural types. As the spheres of work and daily life are reintegrated, we can logically expect that the sharp distinctions between the traditional architectural types will continue to become less definitive.

DOMESTICITY

In describing typical representations from the first half of the nineteenth century of German private houses, the historian Alexandra Richie mentions "images of pretty but not grand interiors, of young men in their libraries or young ladies practising the piano or having tea or singing Christmas carols. The rooms were cosy and homely, with wooden floors and striped silk wallpaper, filled with dainty furniture of lavender and cherrywood. The centre of this world was the family."[56] The comfort of the houses suggested by Richie's words, and the orderliness and functionality that would have maintained them, were not spontaneous inventions of an architect. Rather, they represent highly refined attitudes that could scarcely have developed if it were not for the fact that for over two centuries the intellectual and physical capabilities of bourgeois European women and their later middle-class American counterparts had been channeled toward the near-exclusive responsibility of tending their houses and caring for their families.

Rybczynski describes Dutch painter Emanuel de Witte's seventeenth-century paintings of women within their homes (fig. 16): "It was natural for women to be the focus of de Witte's paintings, because the domestic world that he was depicting had become *their* realm. The world of male work, and male social life, had moved elsewhere. The house had become the place for another kind of work—specialized domestic work—women's work. This work itself was nothing new, but its isolation was."[57] Within this isolation, daily activities—the preparation and serving of meals, the raising and education of children, the furnishing of the house and the arrangement of its contents—were transformed, achieving a near ritual status. Under the supervision of its mistress, the private house became, rather than simple shelter, an environment dedicated to the physical and psychological comforts we associate with the term domesticity.[58]

It must be remembered that, despite its widespread popularity over the centuries, the private house and all it has come to represent have not been without their critics. Charles Baudelaire's flaneur, the urban-dwelling man of the boulevards and the antithesis of the proper bourgeois gentleman, appeared, unsurprisingly, at the same time the cult of the domestic was exerting tremendous influence over French culture. André Gide's contemporaneous words were even more strident: "Families, I hate you! Closed shutters, sealed doors, happiness jealously guarded."[59]

The critics of middle-class life in America have turned not to the boulevards but to the highway, from Walt Whitman's "Song of the Open Road" (1856) to Jack Kerouac's *On The Road* (1957). Feminist voices have also seized upon the hermetic quality of the private house and the limited horizons it has presented to women, from Henrik Ibsen's *A Doll's House* (1879) to Joyce Carol Oates's "Where Are You Going, Where Have You Been?" (1974).

While the aforementioned literary critiques by virtue of their eloquence have been the most pointed, architects and clients themselves have contributed to the discussion. In some instances, such as Peter Eisenman's House VI (Cornwall, Connecticut, 1972–75), the critique is quite evident and specific. Stairs that lead nowhere suggest the claustrophobia so many feminists associate with the

FIGURE 16: *Emanuel de Witte*. Interior with a Woman Playing the Virginal. *c. 1660.*
Paint on canvas, 30½ x 41⅛" (77.5 x 104.5 cm).
Loan: The Netherlands Institute of Cultural Heritage, Rijswijk. Location: Museum Boijmans Van Beuningen, Rotterdam

FIGURE 17: *Clorindo Testa, Architect. Ghirardo-Kohen House, Buenos Aires. 1994. View of original moldings with alterations*

FIGURE 18: *Gordon Matta-Clark. Splitting. 1974. Cibachrome, 30 x 40" (76.2 x 101.6 cm). Courtesy of the Estate of Gordon Matta-Clark and David Zwirner, New York*

private house. A column inconveniently interrupts the dining–room space, becoming a silent presence at the table and creating a sense of tension. The twin beds in the master bedroom were originally separated by a gap in the floor, creating a psychological distance despite the obvious proximity.[60]

Testa's Ghirardo–Kohen House, a complete reconfiguration of a grand suburban residence north of Buenos Aires, might equally be interpreted as a critique of the cult of domesticity. Built in the 1920s, the original house was designed in a Tudor style, the very image of the house as an institution devoted to tradition and comfort. Testa's design deconstructs this image, with slashing interventions that slice through the house and open it up (fig. 17). Along with these excisions, which recall the work of the artist Gordon Matta–Clark (fig. 18), Testa expanded the house by adding to it strange new forms that are as disquieting and inexplicable as the original house's imagery was soothing and familiar.

Similarly, Koolhaas's Maison à Bordeaux strikes an unsentimental pose in opposition to traditional expressions of domesticity. Perhaps Herbert Muschamp, the *New York Times* architecture critic, has described it best as "a shelter from shelter."[61] Denari's resolutely aloof design for the Massey House might be discussed in the same terms. This aloofness is, in a sense, a kind of antidomesticity, a highly stylized, constitutional unfamiliarity that is both challenging and liberating.

Other houses might be cited that do not necessarily reject domesticity per se, but certainly avoid the evocation of any traditional visions of domesticity. Designs such as the T–House, Bell's Glass House @ 2°, and Craig Konyk's Luini House (fig. 19) may not elicit the same sense of the profoundly unfamiliar that characterizes Koolhaas's and Denari's houses. Yet they are adamantly unsentimental—particularly when compared to the ersatz classicism of postmodern domestic architecture—in rejecting any sort of allusion to traditional house design.

Whether any of the houses presented in this book aspires to the physical and psychological comforts of domesticity, the question still remains: who is going to perform the work that creates these comforts? By the end of World War II, opportunities for women to work outside the home, out of choice or necessity, were such that approximately thirty percent of women were in the United States labor force. Since then, that number has leapt to sixty percent and now shows no sign of diminishing.[62]

Perhaps the loss, or at least diminishment, of the traditional concept of domesticity is the price that has to be paid to insure that men and women have equal opportunities to develop their talents in both public and private spheres. Who would at this point in time insist that there is a real alternative to this proposition? Yet this raises even more questions. If the private house no longer has a domestic character, what sort of character will it have?

The easiest solution may be to simply look beyond the domestic status quo (or at this point, perhaps the status quo ante would be more appropriate), as the architect and owners of the Hergott Shepard Residence have done. The two gay men who commissioned the house were intent that its design would reflect their own needs rather than any existing notion of domesticity. In Wright's idealized plan for A Home in a Prairie Town of 1900, "a certain well-established order" underlies the kitchen/pantry/dining–room arrangement. In Maltzan's plan, a new kind of order has been created. The kitchen is noticeably small for the size of the house, reflecting the fact that neither of the owners cooks on a regular basis. However, the kitchen is placed adjacent to the garage, which doubles as a set-up space used by catering services for, among other things, the many fund-raising events the men host for political causes. The owners conceived of the central living areas as public spaces for these events. As they have a large art collection, this public space has also been designed to serve as a gallery with two distinct spaces appropriate to the scale of the works in their collection.

Other variations on the traditional house plan have been made to accommodate the owners' way of living, from the provision of separate offices at opposite ends of the house to adjacent shower stalls in the master bathroom. As the owners do not plan to have children, the upper level contains only the single bedroom/bath/dressing suite and one of the offices. The rest of the house is principally at ground level, with the loftlike spaces flowing rather easily one into another. The largest room, with the best view, is the gymnasium.

Maltzan's design for the Hergott Shepard Residence may be an implicit critique of traditional domesticity, but it is much more about thoughtfully and articulately seeking an alternative. In this sense, the house reflects a long-standing American attitude toward the private house and its design. In describing Catherine E. Beecher's *A Treatise on Domestic Economy for the Use of Young Ladies at Home and at School* of 1841, Rybczynski points out that its early discussion of the planning and building of domestic architecture in America was not written by an architect: "Beecher was expressing a point of view that had not been heard since the seventeenth century in Holland—that of the user. This was the prime characteristic of American domesticity."[63] While the qualities of the average family may change, Maltzan's design reflects a continuing belief that the best design, the only logical design, for a house is one that reflects its owner's needs and desires. Indeed, the designs for all the houses presented in this book do not claim, as have so many model homes in the past, to be new paradigms for living. Rather, they are responses to specific needs.

At this point, it is interesting to reintroduce the topic of the loft. If the spatial structure of the traditional house derives from the ritualization of certain domestic activities, such as the preparation and serving of meals and the receiving of guests, the loft's absence of structure is notable. While the relative openness and flexibility of the loft have inherent spatial and visual pleasures, the appeal of the loft is not simply aesthetic. Choosing the unstructured space of a "New York loft set in Santa Barbara" over a traditional house might also be seen as a desire to live in a house that more accurately reflects the domestic patterns of contemporary living, whether the inhabitants are single people, couples, or families with children.

No longer a "found" space, the loft-type structure has become an alternative to the one-, two-, or three-bedroom private house for a variety of reasons. Designed for couples with children, the Glass House @ 2° and the Slot/Box house by Daly Genik (fig. 20) are similar in their flowing, unstructured interiors, their long, narrow footprints that exaggerate the sense of distance within, and their untraditional appearance compared to their neighbors. Mastenbroek's and MVRDV's Double House and Steven Holl's Y House (pp. 140–43) in New York State remind us that the loft-type house is more an attempt to re-create the openness and lack of rigid structure of an industrial

FIGURE 19: *KONYKarchitecture. Luini House, Long Island, New York. 1997–99*

FIGURE 20: *Daly Genik. Slot/Box, Santa Monica. 1998*

loft rather than its form. In this sense, the Double House might be considered a vertical loft, and the Y House a loft that is folded onto itself. These projects are also evidence that a New York loft in Santa Barbara, or anywhere else for that matter, is not necessarily an oxymoron. Even so, their emphasis on open, flowing spaces is no less than a reversal of the prescriptions for domesticity in *La Maison de Kant*: "stability and finitude, not openness and infinity."[64]

Some recent examples not only invert that emphasis on stability but also make a relative virtue of instability. In the Ost/Kuttner Apartment, the dining room virtually disappears when the table is folded up into a partition. Similarly, the Ghirardo–Kohen House and the Holley Loft can be transformed to accommodate various social situations, from hosting formal dinner parties to housing overnight guests, by a complex series of sliding and pivoting walls and disappearing doors. De Menil's Shorthand House, with its movable partitions, reflects the play between the French word for office, *cabinet*, and the English sense of the same word, which refers to a piece of furniture with sliding drawers and pivoting doors. In the architect's words, "What defines one space from another are things that move."[65]

In the Maison à Bordeaux, major architectural elements can be manipulated. The entire twenty-five-foot-long glass facade of the main living level can be moved away electronically to transform the spaces into an open-air room. Furthermore, installed in the ceiling of the main living space is a series of tracks that allows sliding sunscreens to control the amount of light, hanging works of art to be moved from place to place, and a variety of richly textured fabrics to be positioned to change the atmosphere. Similarly, the structure of Donna Selene Seftel's and William Wilson's 1992 Culebra House project for Culebra, Puerto Rico (fig. 21) is composed of over thirty Dutch doors and a sliding glass wall, all of which can be manipulated to change the interior spaces and to accommodate sun, airflow, privacy, and security.

Recalling the moving partitions of Gerrit Rietveld's Schröder House (Utrecht, The Netherlands, 1924) and the mechanical character of the architectural fittings and furnishings of Chareau's Maison de Verre, we cannot consider the idea of moving parts a recent invention. However, at a time when so many aspects of contemporary life—occupation, residency, personal relationships—seem more transient than permanent, a changeable interior might be as much a metaphoric statement as a functional one.[66]

THE PRIVATE HOUSE: AN ARCHITECTURAL BELLWETHER

While it might be said that the private house is just now beginning to catch up to the fundamental social and cultural changes of recent years, if not decades, the private houses discussed here can also be seen as both a collective bellwether of the current state of architecture and a harbinger of its future direction. Throughout history, the private house has played this role. Unlike larger projects, which normally require broader societal, corporate, or political consensus, the private house can be realized through the efforts of a very few people. It often expresses, in the most uncompromising way possible, the vision of a client or architect, or both.

In this sense, the houses discussed here reflect what have emerged as the two most influential areas of contemporary architectural theory. While they need not necessarily be seen together as a dialectic, these areas of study are

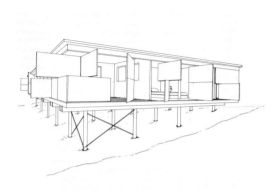

FIGURE 21: *Donna Selene Seftel with William Wilson. Culebra House, Culebra, Puerto Rico. Project, 1992. Exterior perspective*

FIGURE 22: *Möbius strip. Drawing by Paul Bourke*

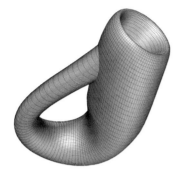

FIGURE 23: *Klein bottle. Drawing by Paul Bourke*

often characterized that way. Moreover, they are all too frequently seen as antipodes in a partisan polemic. This latter view is most accurately summed up in the oft-cited conjunction of mutually derisive terms: "blobs" versus "boxes." The term blob refers to the results of new architectural investigations into various geometric models. Ignoring traditional sources of architectural form, these investigations are based on topology, a branch of mathematics concerned with certain geometries such as the torus, the more complex Möbius strip (fig. 22), and the related Klein bottle (fig. 23) and projective plane.[67]

The Ost/Kuttner Apartment and the more recent Raybould House addition (figs. 24, 25), also by Kolatan and Mac Donald, might serve as examples of the architectonic possibilities of such a topological approach. In both, various spaces are defined to satisfy programmatic needs without interrupting the continuous flow of surfaces. The use of the computer for generating the forms as well as fabricating their fiberglass shells is remarkable in several regards. First, technologies that were previously only available for very large and expensive projects are more accessible, even to relatively small architectural practices; this accessibility is certainly driving much of the interest in complex geometries. Secondly, the physical characteristics of fiberglass make it particularly suitable to the fabrication of complicated, curving shapes. The liquid state of the material during the casting process assures that the resultant surfaces warp and bend as called for in the design and that the final surface is extremely smooth, conveying little sense of texture or scale. The result, as can be seen in Kolatan's and Mac Donald's projects, is an environment of liquid spatiality; the Raybould House in particular becomes what architect and critic Jeffrey Kipnis has called a "meditation on the architecture of the structural skin."[68]

A number of their peers, such as Greg Lynn and Alejandro Zaera-Polo, are perhaps more closely associated with these investigations into complex geometry through their well-known designs for, respectively, the Korean Presbyterian Church of New York in Sunnyside, Queens (1995–98; with Douglas Garofalo and Michael McInturf) and the Yokohama International Port Terminal (competition proposal 1995, projected completion 2002). Nonetheless, if history is a guide, it should be no surprise that among the most advanced realizations of the complex, seamless geometries that had until recently been largely theoretical are Kolatan's and Mac Donald's relatively modest apartment and their house addition.

Many questions, of course, remain as to how these new technologies will be deployed, particularly on a larger scale. Yet the most important questions are not technical but philosophical. What is it about topology that has captured

FIGURE 24: *Kolatan/Mac Donald Studio. Raybould House and Garden, Fairfield County, Connecticut. 1997–99. Exterior perspective. Computer-generated image by Kolatan/Mac Donald Studio*

FIGURE 25: *Kolatan/Mac Donald Studio. Raybould House and Garden, Fairfield County, Connecticut. 1997–99. Interior perspective. Computer-generated image by Kolatan/Mac Donald Studio*

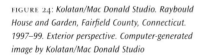

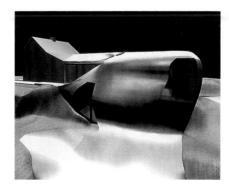

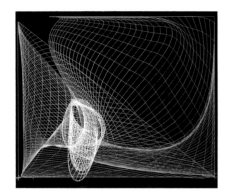

FIGURE 26: *Stephen Perrella with Rebecca Carpenter, Hypersurface Systems, Inc. Möbius House. Project, 1998. Site diagram*

FIGURE 27: *Alejandro Zaera-Polo, Foreign Office Architects. Virtual House. Project, 1997. Exterior perspective. Computer-generated image*

FIGURE 28: *Waro Kishi. House in Shimogamo, Kyoto. 1994*

FIGURE 29: *Sean Godsell. Kew House, Melbourne, Australia. 1997*

the imagination of so many architects who have created so many projects that simply could not have existed a decade ago? In the case of private houses, Cohen's Torus House, van Berkel's Möbius House, Stephen Perrella's and Rebecca Carpenter's Möbius House (fig. 26), and Zaera–Polo's Virtual House (fig. 27) all take their primary form, and in three of the four cases even their names, from topological geometries. Yet in each of these works, the scale of the organizational problem underlying the private house can hardly justify the use of such complex geometries.

Their appeal is, it must be acknowledged, in part aesthetic and in part technological. There is a novelty to these new forms and the means of creating them that is compelling as well as beautiful and marvelous. Nonetheless, the real interest in using these geometries on a domestic scale lies in the connections that can be drawn between them and broader cultural issues. If, as we have seen, the "un–private house" has challenged many of the dialectics that had calcified around the concept of the private house during the nineteenth century—public/private, male/female, nature/culture, and so on—topology takes the challenge further in that it is inherently disposed to creating spatial interconnections rather than making spatial distinctions. In other words, the Möbius strip, which has neither inside nor outside, seems to bear little relationship to the world described in *La Maison de Kant*, a world that was defined by dialectical differences. However, Haraway's cyborg might easily be imagined to be ensconced in Zaera–Polo's Virtual House, which shifts "constantly between a lining and a wrapping condition,"[69] a quality that seems suited to the cyborg's "partiality, irony, intimacy, and perversity."

If the philosophical attitude underlying the use of single–surface geometries can be described as nondialectical, the distinctions between architectural interior and exterior stand to be diminished as much as any other opposition. The idea that the interior of an architectural object might be continuous with its exterior has opened up enormous possibilities for contemporary design. In the site plans for Kolatan's and Mac Donald's Raybould House, the amorphous forms of the house are part of a landscape of equally amorphous shapes. In a somewhat different strategy, the BV House lies close to the earth, its horizontally configured forms appearing to mimic tectonic plates. De Geyter's House in Brasschaat and van Berkel's Villa Wilbrink (Amersfoort, The Netherlands, 1994), among others, narrow the difference between landscape and architecture by treating the surfaces of the latter as part of the former.

Behind every "blob" is the figure of August Möbius, the German mathematician who first published the single–sided figure named after him in 1865. It can also be argued that the "box" has its own paternity. It is difficult to dissociate the term, however obvious it may sound, from the pivotal work of Mies van der Rohe. The relatively unheralded reemergence of the influence of Mies at the end of the twentieth century deserves note. Despite the incredible breadth of his production, conservative architectural critics such as Vincent Scully dubbed him the author of what they derisively and reductively referred to as the "glass box." Far from being a pariah today, the "glass box" has reappeared in such diverse and far–flung residential projects as Group's Leisure Studio in Espoo, Finland (1992), Waro Kishi's House in Shimogamo (fig. 28), Sean Godsell's Kew House (fig. 29), and Bell's Glass House @ 2°. In more complex and fragmentary ways, other projects considered here, including

Maltzan's Hergott Shepard Residence, de Geyter's House in Brasschaat, and Sejima's and Nishizawa's M House, similarly echo, or at least refer to, Mies's seminal steel-and-glass works.

The fin-de-siècle reappearance of Mies is as dramatic as it is unexpected. Twenty years ago, Mies's ideas, and modernism in general, were considered a spent force, a judgment summed up rather neatly by Stanley Tigerman's collage depicting Mies's 1950–56 Crown Hall sinking, Titanic-like, into the waters of Lake Michigan (fig. 30). Mies's reemergence is not, it should be noted, due to revived cadres of adherents revving up the old war cries like "less is more" and "God is in the details." The evidence suggests that the pervasiveness of Mies's influence today is precisely due to the extent to which it has finally escaped the rhetorical sloganeering with which it had become encrusted. If a great number of younger architects have found Mies's legacy to be so fertile, it may be because they no longer need the master's or his disciples' permission to use it. They are no more "Miesian" than Andrea Palladio was "Albertian"; they have simply absorbed this century's great architectural lessons without letting the architect absorb them.

Some of the greatest revisions in our perception of Mies's work and, hence, its ability to influence contemporary architecture have been wrought by the near endless quotation and repositioning of the architect's work by Koolhaas and his firm, the Office for Metropolitan Architecture. The first chapter of his magnum opus, *S, M, L, XL*,[70] presents fantastic histories of Mies's Kröller-Müller House project for The Hague (1912) and the Barcelona Pavilion (1929), which precede photographic essays on his own designs: Two Patio Villas (Rotterdam, The Netherlands, 1984–88), Nexus World Housing (Fukuoka, Japan, 1991), and the Villa Dall'Ava (St. Cloud, Paris, 1985–91). In this seminal chapter, Koolhaas's revisionist interpretation of the Barcelona Pavilion, the most modern of architectural icons, is complete, presenting a vision of Mies that is no longer pure, classical, and sober, but queer (or "bent," as he says), Hollywood, and delirious. No longer an object trapped in a distant, unreachable, or perfectible past, the Barcelona Pavilion has been reworked for current consumption; the image of a buff athlete showering in Koolhaas's Two Patio Villas (fig. 31) is what would be called in the film industry a "remake" of Georg Kolbe's cast-bronze maiden captured within the Pavilion's courtyard reflecting pool (fig. 32).

Koolhaas's repositioning of Mies within a postmodern context is not

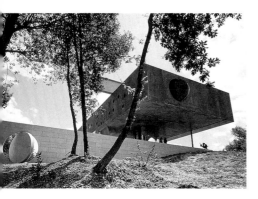

FIGURE 33: *Rem Koolhaas, Office for Metropolitan Architecture. Maison à Bordeaux, France. 1998*

FIGURE 34: *Ludwig Mies van der Rohe. Riehl House, Potsdam. 1907*

simply a literary project. The Maison à Bordeaux is an example of the Office for Metropolitan Architecture's appropriation of numerous Miesian devices in its built work. As with many of Koolhaas's projects, the conceptual starting point is a socle, the platform or plinth that Mies used to elevate to lesser or greater degrees his structures above the earth—a tactic he inherited from the Neoclassical architect Karl Friedrich Schinkel. Another example might be seen in the first view of the building one has from the driveway (fig. 33), which reprises the famous garden view of Mies's earliest house, the Riehl House (fig. 34). In addition, the rear facade (fig. 35) clearly echoes the profile of Mies's cantilevered Glass House on Hillside project of 1934 (fig. 36).

The work of Herzog and de Meuron has also contributed enormously to the revitalization of interest in Mies's work. Projects such as their Koechlin House (fig. 37) remind us that, above all, architectonics is a visual and ultimately sensual discipline; only secondarily is it a technical one. In this sense, the detailing of the flush plaster, glass, and metal surfaces in the Koechlin House is emblematic of the technical rigor required to execute such a building, yet it is only fully appreciated on a visual level. The absolute juxtaposition of the materials, held tautly in plane, heightens our awareness of them, their physical differences and their unexpected similarities. Although Mies's work, as his reputation retreated after his death, came to be widely derided as austere and culturally errant, the product of determinist forces, this project and others show us how *for the same reasons* Miesian can also mean sensuous, subjective, and replete with specifically local conditions.

While Herzog and de Meuron and Koolhaas have managed to get us to look at the architect's work differently, other events have helped us to see Mies's work on his own terms. Two of his most important built works, the Barcelona Pavilion, which was demolished in 1930, and the Tugendhat House in Brno, Czech Republic (1928–30), which was damaged and severely altered during and after World War II and then became virtually inaccessible during the Cold War, are accessible again. The pavilion was rebuilt in 1986, and the villa was partially restored in recent years. Both are open to the public and have come alive for an entire generation of architects who have only known them through the historical chasm that black-and-white photography can suggest. San Francisco architect Stanley Saitowitz's description of his visit to the rebuilt pavilion suffices to describe the profundity of experiencing this previously lost masterwork of Mies's early career: "Visiting

FIGURE 35: *Rem Koolhaas, Office for Metropolitan Architecture. Maison à Bordeaux, France. 1998*

FIGURE 36: *Ludwig Mies van der Rohe. Glass House on Hillside. Project, 1934. Elevation sketch. Ink on paper, 4¼ x 8" (10.7 x 20.3 cm). The Museum of Modern Art, New York. Mies van der Rohe Archive*

FIGURE 37: *Herzog & de Meuron. Koechlin House, Basel. 1994*

FIGURE 38: *Bernard Tschumi. Glass Video Gallery, Groningen, The Netherlands. 1990*

the Pavilion, I realize what space is, and experience what a fish may when it first grasps that it lives in water.... Being inside makes me float, and I take huge breaths, filling my lungs with air."[71]

The point to be made here is not that the Maison à Bordeaux, or any of the other houses discussed here, is simply a sum total of a number of Miesian references. In Herzog's and de Meuron's Kramlich Residence, for example, the overall form of the work is clearly indebted to Mies; the hovering roof sheltering a glass enclosure is part Barcelona Pavilion, part Farnsworth House. Yet the interior configuration and the programmatic elements are something altogether different. When completed, the lower level of the house will provide space for semipermanent video installations, and the undulating, semitransparent walls of the living quarters will be rendered immaterial by the flickering presence of digital images.

It might be argued that the revived interest in the glass house and its spatial conditions is, paradoxically, an indication of how much culture has changed since Mies's time. Conceived as a heroically contemplative place, the Farnsworth House met with great public resistance for the simple fact that it was assumed one could see in as easily as see out. This visual accessibility flew in the face of accepted notions of privacy at the time. At the end of the twentieth century, it might even be said that the "interactive" aspect that was so objectionable previously is now its greatest allure, and that the reflexive gaze of the electronic media has become a metaphor grafted onto the glass box. The shift from machine to media, or perhaps even Mies to Microsoft, can be traced through such projects as Tschumi's Glass Video Gallery (fig. 38), Diller's and Scofidio's Slow House, and Joel Sanders's Kyle Residence project intended for Houston (1993). The Glass Video Gallery, while not an actual house, is a deconstruction and reformulation of the archetypal glass house. While Mies's Farnsworth House came to be called a glass house, it is actually, as Tschumi reminds us, a steel house with a glass skin and is as much a study in the verities of structure as anything else. Tschumi's Glass Video Gallery not only is skewed out of plane, undermining any notion of stability, but the building's columns and beams are structural glass, blurring the distinction between support and surface. A further blurring can be seen in the reflections of the video monitors, ricocheting about the space on various glass surfaces and rendering the architecture as less material and more media.

The reformulation of high European modernism under way today in Europe—led by Herzog and de Meuron, Koolhaas, and Tschumi and their former employees, students, and collaborators such as de Geyter, Annette Gigon and Mike Guyer, and Maas—is certainly not its first major revision. This reevaluation, of which Mies plays so critical a part, owes a large debt to those transformations of prewar modernism initially engendered by Richard Neutra and later Charles and Ray Eames, Pierre Koenig, and the other architects selected by John Entenza for the Case Study Program houses, begun after 1945 and built in Southern California (figs. 39, 40). In these years, Los Angeles became a crucible for the definition of a postwar culture of modernity that blended the original impulses of European modernism with the divergent strands of Yankee pragmatism and California sensuality.

The work of a number of younger California architects who have recently established practices, among them Michael Maltzan Architecture,

FIGURE 39: *Charles and Ray Eames. Eames House, Pacific Palisades, California. 1945–49*

FIGURE 40: *Pierre Koenig. Case Study House 22, Los Angeles. 1959*

Guthrie + Buresh Architects, and Daly Genik—although each of these studios traces its lineage through Frank O. Gehry's office—shows the ongoing influence of the architects of the Case Study houses. The same could be said of other Los Angeles–based practices, such as Angelil/Graham, Central Office of Architecture, Koning Eizenberg Architecture, Thom Mayne, and Michael Rotondi, as well as offices further afield. Even so, the ongoing reinterpretations of California modernism evident in the work of these architects is not taking place within a closed circle. Herzog and de Meuron, Koolhaas, and Coop Himmelb(l)au, all of whom are active in California, continue to contribute a European view of America's new Eden—as did their predecessors Neutra, Rudolph Schindler, and Albert Frey—even as they draw from its unique blend of contemporary and historical sources.

A similar assessment might be made of the process by which European modernism metamorphosed within a Japanese cultural context. In the work of Toyo Ito, Kishi, Sejima, and many others, it is possible to see a parallel recasting of Mies and other Western modernists as less formal, more tactile, and more transient in a way that cannot be fully explained by modernism's European roots. Many ideological purists once considered these cross-cultural hybrids—California, to the east of the Pacific Rim, and Japan, to the west—a dilution of the original manifestos of the early twentieth century. Yet they represent today one of the greatest resources for the ongoing transformation of modern architecture.

THE UN-PRIVATE HOUSE

Certain conclusions can be drawn about the status of the private house at the end of the century, both as a cultural invention and as a product of the autonomous discipline of architecture. All the houses examined in this book depart substantially from the patterns established by the traditional private house. Furthermore, it is interesting to note their many similarities to the medieval hall, the traditional private house's antecedent. For example, large, open spaces, rather than cellular divisions of rooms, characterize both the "big houses" and contemporary lofts or loftlike houses. As such, the main spaces in both frequently have had multiple functions. One of the most important of these functions in the medieval house would have been the performance of work and business activities. The contemporary loftlike living space is similarly associated with work, given its emergence as an alternative home in the 1970s for artists wanting spaces in which to live and work. In the instance of the big house, the strong presence of the public world in the home was a physical one; in the case of what might be called the "unprivate house," it is often a digital presence.

It would be overreaching to suppose that the popularity of the traditional private house is now on the wane, and that eventually it will be bracketed historically by the medieval big house and the contemporary "unprivate house." Indeed, one of the things that has made the private house such an institution has been its applicability and desirability to a large class of people. That class of people still exists and will, no doubt, guarantee a market for private houses that are more traditional than otherwise. Nonetheless, it is manifestly evident that the private house developed for a fairly static nuclear family is not necessarily applicable to all householders or even a majority of them.

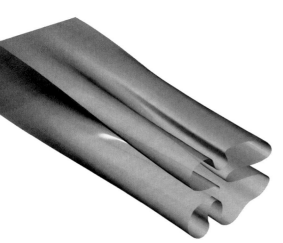

FIGURE 41: *Ben van Berkel,
UN Studio/Van Berkel & Bos, in
collaboration with Cecil Balmond,
Ove Arup & Partners. "Octopus"
conceptual model for Haus für Musik
und Musiktheater, Graz, Austria.
Design 1998, projected completion 2002*

Various scenarios for the future might be considered. If the housing industry responds to the changing conditions discussed herein as they have already responded to the needs of the growing elderly population throughout most of the industrialized world, it is possible that in the future the market will offer an increased number of housing types. Or a strategy could easily be adopted by both architects and the building industry to make a more rigorous distinction between structural and programmatic elements in the planning and construction of houses, which would allow for a transformation of houses over time as owners' situations change. It may also be that various technologies currently being developed to tailor consumer goods to buyers' individual needs will be applied to the home-building industry. Just as Herman Miller's Aeron office chair (1992) comes, like a piece of clothing, in small, medium, and large sizes, a "custom" house might be made available to a broader segment of society.

The dynamics of the real-estate market and the building industry will also, no doubt, experience great changes as a significant number of people no longer have separate work and living places. The impact of this shift is not clear. Perhaps members of the middle class will have more money to spend on their single places of work and living. Or will other patterns emerge? Could it be that it will become more common for people to spend less on their homes-workplaces and save their earnings to buy weekend houses, thereby reintegrating solitude into an otherwise wired world?

These changes in themselves will not automatically generate an appropriate architecture. Rather it will be, as it has been for centuries, the role of the architect to interpret these changes into built form. While the adherents of "boxes" as well as those who support "blobs" can claim a vision of the future, neither strategy—if these approaches can be called that—will have a significant impact upon the course of architectural development if it is defined in formal terms alone. The current debate between those who are investigating either the ongoing possibilities for prismatic architecture or the newer, more complex geometries calls to mind Leonardo da Vinci's High Renaissance writings in which he speculated on the nature of form. By his reasoning, there were two types of visible bodies: "The first is without shape or any distinct or definite extremities.... The second kind... is that of which the surface defines and distinguishes the shape."[72]

The computer has, of course, made the absolute distinctions that Leonardo saw between simpler and more complex geometries unsustainable. Simple, rectilinear geometries and curving topologies (with the exception of certain "nonorientable" geometries) are now more accurately seen as points on a sliding scale of complexity rather than as fundamentally different types of forms. In designs such as van Berkel's and Cecil Balmond's Haus für Musik und Musiktheater (fig. 41), Cohen's Torus House, and Kolatan and Mac Donald's Ost/Kuttner Apartment, newly accessible geometries and more familiar ones are fused within continua of form.

If simpler and more complex geometries can be understood as more similar than dissimilar, then we can also see that attempts to judge one or the other superior on a formal basis alone are not supportable. These attempts simply maintain the misunderstanding that Leonardo and his contemporaries shared. In the instance of the Torus House, the fusion of the normative glass box and the torus forces a suspension of all the associations imputed to one form or the other. The compressed horizontality of its space recalls the Cartesian infinitude ascribed to Mies's work; the remnants of the torus form at its center suggest its own, internalized kind of endlessness. The fusion of the two, although generated from dissimilar mathematical models, creates a tandem sense of the boundless, both from without and within.

In a similar way, Glass House @ 2° forces us to rethink standard formalistic histories. Bell's design, with its obvious references to Mies's work, is a prismatic volume that is slightly and intentionally distorted, as if it had been pinched. In a strictly formalist reading, one might be tempted to conclude that because it is distorted it therefore can no longer be considered Miesian. But the opposite is true: the essential Miesian characteristic that defines the project, its sense of boundlessness, cannot be accurately and completely defined solely by form.

This is not to say that form is irrelevant or that all geometries are alike. Rather, it is crucial to note that dissimilar forms are not necessarily ideologically oppositional and that formal distinctions in architecture are not the most important ones. For example, as we go forward into an era of great cultural and technological change, the conception of the architectural surface as a skin in which information is imbedded, as in the Kramlich Residence, The Digital House, and the Hyper House Pavilion 5, is a much more intriguing and critical point of departure than their obvious differences in geometric form.

The cultural definition of the private house is undergoing great change, a transformation that, in itself, can generate significant architectural invention. This change is taking place at a time when architecture is being fueled by enormous new technical and material resources. The private houses discussed here, and the architects who designed them, can thus be seen as not only reconfiguring the domestic landscape but laying the groundwork for the first architectural debates of the twenty-first century. In the cultural imagination and in the mind of the architect, the landscape of the built environment remains linked to what Hélion called "the problem of the house."

1 Jean Hélion, "Termes de vie, termes d'espace," *Cahiers d'art* 10, nos. 7–10 (1935), p. 268.

2 For a more thorough history of the origins and development of the private house, see Matthew Johnson, *Housing Culture: Traditional Architecture in an English Landscape* (Washington, D.C.: Smithsonian Institution Press, 1993); Amos Rapoport, *House Form and Culture* (Englewood Cliffs, N.J.: Prentice-Hall, 1969); and Witold Rybczynski, *Home: A Short History of an Idea* (New York: Penguin Books, 1986).

3 From the first definition in *Merriam-Webster's Collegiate Dictionary*, 10th ed. (Springfield, Mass.: Merriam-Webster, 1995), p. 927.

4 Quoted in Michelle Perrot, "At Home," in Perrot, ed., *A History of Private Life*, vol. 4, From the Fires of Revolution to the Great War, trans. Arthur Goldhammer (Cambridge, Mass.: Harvard University Press, Belknap Press, 1990), p. 342. From Bernard Edelman, *La Maison de Kant* (Paris: Payot, 1984), pp. 25–26.

5 Letter from Thomas Jefferson to Baron Geismar, Sept. 6, 1785, in Albert Ellery Bergh, ed., *The Writings of Thomas Jefferson*, vol. 5 (Washington, D.C.: The Thomas Jefferson Memorial Association of the United States, 1907), pp. 128–29.

6 While not a comprehensive survey, a cursory look into national databases confirms this. In Sweden, Switzerland, and France, for example, private houses account for forty-six, fifty-four, and fifty-six percent of the housing stock, respectively. See Statistiska centralbyrån (Statistics Sweden), "Housing: Dwellings by Type" (http://www.scb.se/scbeng/svsiffror/svsiffrorbostadeng.htm); Swiss Federal Statistical Office (Neuchâtel), "9 Construction and Housing: Features of Housing 1990" (http://www.admin.ch/bfs/stat_ch/ber09/eu0905.htm); and National Institute of Statistics and Economic Studies (INSEE; France), "Living Standard: Automobiles, Housing" (http://www.insee.fr/va/keyfigur/fb008_a.htm). All World Wide Web sources cited in this essay were accessible in April 1999.

7 U.S. Census Bureau, "Housing Starts and Building Permits in July 1998," *Building Online: U.S. Census Bureau Housing Starts*, released Aug. 19, 1998 (http://www.buildingonline.com/housingstarts.htm).

8 Statistics Canada, "Households by Dwelling Characteristics" (http://www.statcan.ca/english/Pgdb/People/Families/famil09.htm).

9 Spiro Kostof, *A History of Architecture: Settings and Rituals* (New York: Oxford University Press, 1985), p. 361. See also chapter 2, "Intimacy and Privacy," in Rybczynski, *Home*.

10 Walter Benjamin, *Reflections: Essays, Aphorisms, Autobiographical Writings*, trans. Edmund Jephcott, ed. Peter Demetz (New York: Schocken Books, 1978), p. 154.

11 Quoted in Michelle Facos, "The Ideal Swedish Home: Carl Larsson's Lilla Hyttnäs," in Christopher Reed, ed., *Not at Home: The Suppression of Domesticity in Modern Art and Architecture* (London: Thames and Hudson, 1996), pp. 81–91.

12 Martin Heidegger, "The Thing," in Heidegger, *Poetry, Language, Thought*, trans. Albert Hofstadter (1971; softcover, New York: Harper & Row, 1975), p. 166. (From essay in German published 1954.)

13 "Results of the Shinkenchiku Residential Design Competition 1991," *JA: The Japan Architect* 5, no. 1 (winter 1992), issue titled *Results: Another Glass House, 1991 Annual*, p. 30.

14 Martin Heidegger, *Being and Time*, trans. John Macquarrie and Edward Robinson (San Francisco: HarperSanFrancisco, 1962), p. 140. (From the seventh German edition; first published 1927.)

15 Diller + Scofidio, unpublished project description, 1990.

16 Beatriz Colomina, "The Exhibitionist House," in *At the End of the Century: One Hundred Years of Architecture* (Los Angeles: The Museum of Contemporary Art; New York: Harry N. Abrams, 1998), p. 158. Colomina's text focuses on exhibition houses, which were designed primarily for display at museums, expositions, or other settings rather than for actual inhabitation.

17 Neil Gershenfeld, *When Things Start to Think* (New York: Henry Holt and Company, 1999), p. 7.

18 Michael Trudgeon, "Hyper House," unpublished project description, 1998.

19 Donna Haraway, "A Manifesto for Cyborgs: Science, Technology, and Socialist Feminism in the 1980s," *Socialist Review* 15 (no. 2), no. 80 (March–April 1985), p. 67.

20 Hannah Arendt, *The Human Condition* (Chicago: The University of Chicago Press, 1958), p. 28.

21 Ibid., p. 30.

22 Nancy Franklin, "Show and Tell," *The New Yorker* 74, no. 25 (Aug. 24 and 31, 1998), p. 11.

23 Frank Lloyd Wright, "A Home in a Prairie Town," *Ladies' Home Journal*, Feb. 1901, p. 17.

24 Frank Lloyd Wright, "Studies and Executed Buildings," in *Ausgeführte Bauten und Entwürfe von Frank Lloyd Wright* (Berlin: Verlag Ernst Wasmuth, [1910]), n.p. Reprinted in Bruce Brooks Pfeiffer, ed., *Frank Lloyd Wright: Collected Writings* (New York: Rizzoli; Scottsdale, Ariz.: The Frank Lloyd Wright Foundation, 1992), p. 108. The identification of privacy, and hence the private house, with individual liberty has particular resonance in American culture. Nonetheless, the same associations were made, Perrot argues, at the end of the nineteenth century in Europe: "People at all levels of society desired greater intimacy within the family, between husband and wife, and among friends.... One form in which they [those desires] were expressed was a growing reluctance to mingle indiscriminately with neighbors and to accept their restrictions on individual behavior." Perrot, "At Home," p. 355.

25 William Safire, "Nobody's Business," *The New York Times on the Web*, Jan. 8, 1998, Editorial Desk sec.

26 Gershenfeld, *When Things Start to Think*, p. 100.

27 Elizabeth Gordon, "The Threat to the Next America," *House Beautiful* 95, no. 4 (April 1953), p. 127.

28 Ibid., p. 129.

29 Quoted in Joseph A. Barry, "Report on the American Battle between Good and Bad Modern Houses," *House Beautiful* 95, no. 5 (May 1953), p. 270.

30 Quoted in Gordon Kipping, G-TECTS, *Ordinary Diagrams*, 2nd ed. (Los Angeles: Public Access Press at the Southern California Institute of Architecture, 1997), sec. 3.2.

31 Luis Moreno Mansilla and Emilio Tuñón, "El espacio del optimismo: Una conversación con Winy Maas, Jacob van Rijs y Nathalie de Vries/The Space of Optimism: A Conversation with Winy Maas, Jacob van Rijs and Nathalie de Vries," *El croquis* 4, no. 86 (1997), issue devoted to MVRDV, p. 15.

32 The project has been built, but not as designed.

33 Bernard Tschumi, unpublished project description, 1992.

34 Taeg Nishimoto, "Just What Is It That Makes Today's House So Different, So Appealing?—Now," unpublished project description, 1991.

35 Kipping, G-TECTS, *Ordinary Diagrams*, sec. 3.5.

36 Jeroen van Bergeijk, "Public Viewing of a Private Life," *Wired News* (http://www.wired.com/news/news/culture/story/16280.html). Alex van Es's Web site is at www.icepick.com.

37 Leo Tolstoy, *Anna Karenina*, trans. David Magarshack (New York: The New American Library, 1961), p. 17.

38 Quoted in Catherine Hall, "The Sweet Delights of Home," in Michelle Perrot, ed., *A History of Private Life*, vol. 4, From the Fires of Revolution to the Great War, trans. Arthur Goldhammer (Cambridge, Mass.: Harvard University Press, Belknap Press, 1990), p. 74. From General Report, *Census of Great Britain, 1851* (1852), 1, p. xxxvi.

39 Hall, "The Sweet Delights of Home," p. 55.

40 Rybczynski, *Home*, p. 59.

41 Witold Rybczynski, "The Biggest Small Buildings," *Architecture* 87, no. 12 (Dec. 1998), p. 59.

42 U.S. Census Bureau, "Historical Census [1990] of Housing Tables: Living Alone" (http://www.census.gov/hhes/www/housing/census/historic/livalone.html). A cursory search of databases from other industrialized countries indicates similar demographics. In Germany and Switzerland, thirty-five and thirty-two percent of households, respectively, consist of a single occupant. In the United Kingdom, the percentage of one-person households, now twelve percent, has increased by fifty percent since 1974. In Japan, the number of single-person households is also growing rapidly. Twenty-six percent of all households have a single person, a twenty-percent increase in five years. See Statistisches Bundesamt Deutschland (Federal Statistical Office Germany), "Households and Population Development" (http://www.statistik-bund.de/basis/e/pop03.htm); Swiss Federal Statistical Office (Neuchâtel), "1 Population: Households" (http://www.admin.ch/bfs/stat_ch/ber01/eu0105.htm); Government Statistical Service (United Kingdom), "The UK in Figures: Population and Vital Statistics" (http://www.statistics.gov.uk/stats/ukinfigs/pop.htm); and Statistics Bureau and Statistics Center, Management and Coordination Agency of Japan, "Households and Household Members" (http://www.stat.go.jp/1602.htm#jf02–06).

43 Ken Bryson and Lynne M. Casper, U.S. Department of Commerce, Economics, and Statistics Administration, "Household and Family Characteristics: March 1997," Table B, [U.S.] Census Bureau, P20–509, issued April 1998 (http://www.census.gov/population/www/socdemo/hh-fam.html).

44 Joseph Giovannini, "Design Notebook: A House Where Rooms Are a State of Mind," *The New York Times*, Aug. 6, 1998, p. F1.

45 In describing many of the characteristics of the private houses recently designed and constructed, the terms loft and loftlike seem to be indispensable. Yet it has to be acknowledged that the adjective loftlike as a description of so many recent houses is as unsatisfactory as the terms one-, two-, or three-bedroom are for describing traditional houses.

46 Karen D. Stein, "Mack Scogin and Merrill Elam," *Architectural Record* 186, no. 4 (April 1998), p. 138.

47 José Oubrerie, "José Oubrerie/Atelier Wylde-Oubrerie: Miller House," *GA Houses* 35 (July 1992), p. 10.

48 Administration on Aging (a U.S. federal agency), "Living Arrangements of Persons 60+, by Age and Sex: 1990" (http://www.aoa.dhhs.gov/aoa/stats/pophous/table10.html). From U.S. Census Bureau, "1990 Census of Population and Housing: Special Tabulation on Aging," STP 14, tables P32 and P34.

49 For more on this subject, see chapter 4, "People Who Live in Glass Houses: Edith Farnsworth, Ludwig Mies van de Rohe, and Philip Johnson," in Alice T. Friedman, *Women and the Making of the Modern House: A Social and Architectural History* (New York: Harry N. Abrams, 1998), pp. 126–59.

50 John D'Emilio and Estelle B. Freedman, *Intimate Matters: A History of Sexuality in America* (New York: Harper & Row, Publishers, 1988), p. 16.

51 Sanders, "Re-'viewing' the Bachelor Pad," unpublished project description, 1998.

52 Roger-Henri Guerrand, "Private Spaces," in Michelle Perrot, ed., *A History of Private Life*, vol. 4, From the Fires of Revolution to the Great War, trans. Arthur Goldhammer (Cambridge, Mass.: Harvard University Press, Belknap Press, 1990), p. 368.

53 Sanders, "Re-'viewing' the Bachelor Pad."

54 Jim Shahin, "'Working' at Home," *American Way* 32, no. 5 (March 1, 1999), p. 44.

55 Winka Dubbeldam, unpublished project description, 1997.

56 Alexandra Richie, *Faust's Metropolis: A History of Berlin* (New York: Carroll & Graf Publishers, 1998), pp. 116–17.

57 Rybczynski, *Home*, pp. 70–71.

58 For more on the subject of domesticity, see Dolores Hayden, *The Grand Domestic Revolution: A History of Feminist Designs for American Homes, Neighborhoods, and Cities* (Cambridge, Mass.: The MIT Press, 1981); Beatriz Colomina, ed., *Sexuality and Space* (New York: Princeton Architectural Press, 1992); and Reed, ed., *Not at Home*.

59 Quoted in Perrot, "At Home," p. 546.

60 In a recent telephone interview with the author, the clients revealed that they have altered the bedroom because they felt it did not accurately represent their relationship.

61 Herbert Muschamp, "Living Boldly on the Event Horizon," *The New York Times*, Nov. 19, 1998, p. F7.

62 Bureau of Labor Statistics, U.S. Department of Labor, "Table A-1: Employment Status of the Civilian Population by Sex and Age: Women, 20 Years and Over," *Labor Force Statistics from the Current Population Survey*, last modified Feb. 1, 1999 (http://stats.bls.gov/webapps/legacy/cpsatab1.htm). Similar statistics can be found in other areas of the industrialized world. Forty-five percent of the United Kingdom's work force is made up of women; in France, the figure is forty-four percent; in Germany, sixty-three percent of women from the age of fifteen to sixty-five are in the work force or seeking employment. See, respectively, Government Statistical Service (United Kingdom), "The UK in Figures: Employment" (http://www.statistics.gov.uk/stats/ukinfigs/employ.htm); National Institute of Statistics and Economic Studies (INSEE; France) "Employment and Earnings: Employment" (http://www.insee.fr/va/keyfigur/fb012_a.htm); and Statistisches Bundesamt Deutschland (Federal Statistical Office Germany), "Employment" (http://www.statistik-bund.de/basis/e/be03.htm).

63 Rybczynski, *Home*, p. 160.

64 Quoted in Perrot, "At Home," p. 342. From Edelman, *La Maison de Kant*, pp. 25–26.

65 Quoted in Edie Cohen, "The Shorthand House," *Interior Design* 9, no. 8 (Oct. 1998), p. 129.

66 For example, in the United States, young wage earners can expect to change jobs almost nine times before they reach mid-career. See Bureau of Labor Statistics, U.S. Department of Labor, "Table 1: Number of Jobs Held by Individuals Aged 18 to 32 in 1978–95: Individuals Aged 31 to 38 in 1995 by Educational Attainment, Sex, Race, Hispanic Origin, and Age," *National Longitudinal Surveys*, last modified June 25, 1998 (http://stats.bls.gov/news.release/nlsoy.t01.htm). Also, of the 522,300 marriages in the United Kingdom in 1995, forty percent of them were second marriages for one or both parties. See Government Statistical Service (United Kingdom), "The UK in Figures: Population and Vital Statistics" (http://www.statistics.gov.uk/stats/ukinfigs/pop.htm).

67 Topology explores certain basic properties of geometric objects that do not change when they are stretched, twisted, or bent, such as the number of edges (or boundaries) and holes. For more information, see Stephen Barr, *Experiments in Topology* (1964; reprint, New York: Dover Publications, 1989); Bernard Cache, *Earth Moves: The Furnishing of Territories*, trans. Anne Boyman, ed. Michael Speaks (Cambridge, Mass.: The MIT Press, 1995); Gilles Deleuze, *Foucault*, trans. and ed. Seán Hand (Minneapolis: University of Minnesota Press, 1988); and Darcy Wentworth Thompson, *On Growth and Form*, ed. John Tyler Bonner, abridged ed. (Cambridge, England: Cambridge University Press, 1961).

68 Jeffrey Kipnis, conversation with the author, Dec. 21, 1998.

69 Alejandro Zaera [-Polo], "La reformulación del suelo/Reformulating the Ground," *Quaderns*, no. 220 (1998), issue titled *Topografías operativas/Operative Topographies*, p. 40.

70 Office for Metropolitan Architecture, Rem Koolhaas, and Bruce Mau, *S, M, L, XL*, ed. Jennifer Sigler (New York: The Monacelli Press, 1995), p. 49.

71 Stanley Saitowitz, correspondence with the author, June 1986.

72 Leonardo da Vinci, *The Notebooks of Leonardo da Vinci*, ed. and trans. Edward MacCurdy (New York: Reynal & Hitchcock, 1939), pp. 986–87.

Projects

Dates in the project headings indicate the
completion of construction; dates given for
unbuilt houses, however, are those of final
design. See pages 145–49 for more detailed
project information and credits. In the texts
that follow, all quotes and some information have been drawn from descriptions
submitted by the participating architects.

Designed by Winka Dubbeldam, the Millbrook Residence is intended for a thirty-four-acre site atop a hill in the Catskill Mountains. Its clients, a graphic designer and make-up artist who are often involved in international projects, need spaces for living, working, and rest—in sum, a house that will serve as a way station for lives lived on the go.

Dubbeldam has called the Millbrook Residence a "field of three-dimensional movement." She conceived the house as a reconfigured knot whose winding path ascends through the landscape outside and then continues into the house's interior, where it retraces the topography of the hills in upward and downward movements. Spaces for work and living are interwoven, flowing smoothly from one to the next. For example, the upper-level studio, which is the wife's work space, and the living room, are joined.

Dubbeldam's notion of the house as "a kind of antifortress, offering...a way of dwelling that remains open to dynamic and contingent exchanges with its sur-

roundings" is manifest in many forms throughout her design. The media room on the lower level, which is also the husband's workplace, opens the house up to unlimited information accessible through electronic equipment, computer, and modem. Outside, the forms of a stepped ramp, terraces, and a lap pool suggest an endless extension of the house into the landscape. The structure of the house also furthers dynamic exchange. Suspended like a curtain around a light steel framework, lean glass walls minimize the distinctions between inside and out. Visual connections are multiplied indoors, where living areas are folded around voids. These glass-walled spaces, open to the sky, render the house porous. As they mediate space and vision, these voids bring traces of the exterior indoors and reconnect upper and lower levels to the outside through a play of light and reflections.

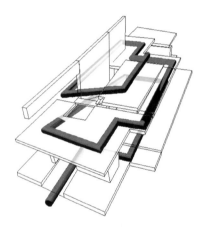

Circulation diagrams

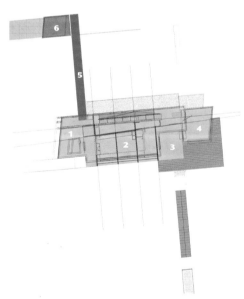

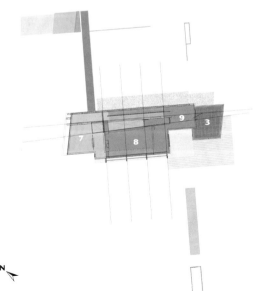

1 *Entry*
2 *Kitchen/dining area*
3 *Terrace*
4 *Media room/work space*
5 *Lap pool*
6 *Guest house*
7 *Bedroom*
8 *Living area*
9 *Work space*

Ground-floor plan

Upper-level plan

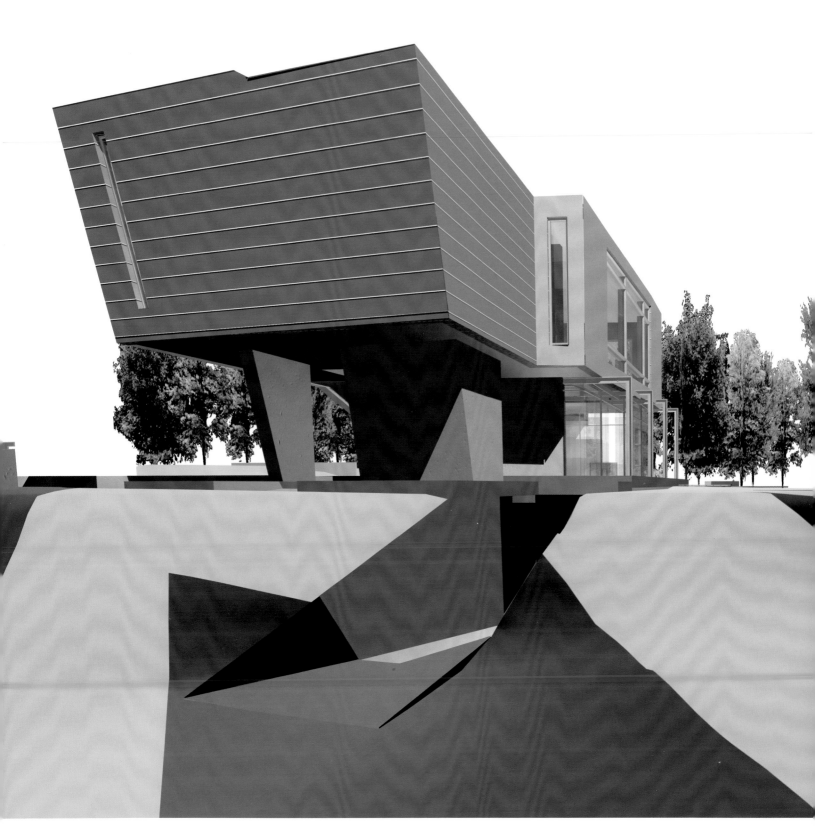

View from northwest. Computer-generated image

View of circulation ramp from upper level.
Computer-generated image

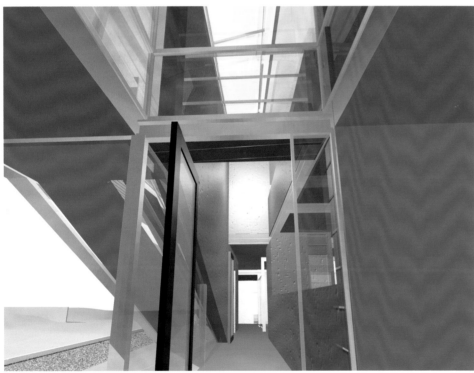

View of entry with circulation ramp at left.
Computer-generated image

View from south. Computer-generated image

The Lipschutz/Jones Apartment in downtown Manhattan was designed by Frank Lupo and Daniel Rowen for a professional couple, currency traders on Wall Street. The clients wanted an apartment with a free plan but also a work space—essentially a digital trading room—that could be viewed from various vantage points within the apartment yet would be remote enough from the bedroom to allow one to work late at night without disturbing the other. The design compresses much of the programmatic requirements into a two-level volume at the back of the apartment, adjacent to the building's internal corridor wall. At the front, along the exterior window wall, is a large, double-height space serving as the living room. A tall, narrow corridor runs from the front to the back and separates the "compressed" program into two distinct halves: on the one side, the kitchen is below with bedroom above, and on the other, the trading and dressing rooms are below with master bath above. The trading room is thus isolated from the bedroom, but can be seen from the kitchen and the main circulation corridor of the apartment. In addition to those in the trading room, six video monitors located throughout the apartment allow the couple to keep track of world financial markets on a twenty-four-hour basis.

A steel ladder gives access to the upper level of the apartment. A cantilevered, steel bridge spans the gap created by the double-height corridor, which also serves as a library. From the bridge, one can look either down on the living room or across to the views of the city framed by the exterior windows. By virtue of its location, the living room acts as a space linking the sculptural interior facades of the apartment's compressed volumes to the facades of the city beyond.

The architects used the technical elements required for the trading floor along with a varied palette of materials, such as maple, slate, marble, granite, frosted glass, and stainless steel, to give the apartment its visual character. The constantly flickering digital screens convey information, but in their placement and framing also assume aesthetic qualities.

1 *Entry*
2 *Living/dining area*
3 *Kitchen*
4 *Digital trading room*
5 *Double-height corridor*
6 *Bedroom*

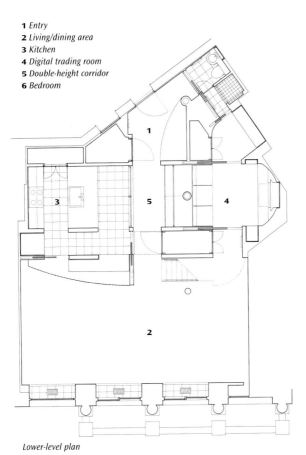

Lower-level plan

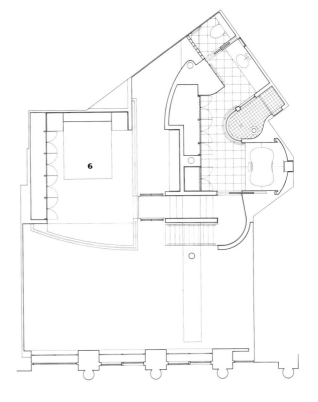

Upper-level plan

View of kitchen through jalousie from double-height corridor

View of digital trading room

Shower enclosure in master bathroom

Designed in 1997–98 by Jacques Herzog and Pierre de Meuron, the Kramlich Residence and Media Collection is to be constructed in Napa Valley among neighboring vineyards. The structure is conceived as both a home for a couple and a place to show their extensive collection of electronic art. The design is characterized by intentional ambiguity: home as media installation, or media installation as home?

Access to the house is by a road that descends to a garage a half level below ground. From the garage, where a forty-seven-foot-long video panorama of Gary Hill's *Viewer* (1996) is to be shown, the visitor will proceed another half level down into the gallery, a much larger underground space that is, in the words of the architects, a "black box brought to life only through the illuminated projections of the artists."

The design's main living areas are above ground, set in an eccentrically

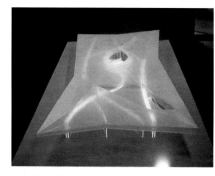

Model from above

shaped glass pavilion. While the spaces are connected by a winding stair that frames a double-height space, the dreamlike world of electronic images below is in contrast to the immediate experience of nature that the glazed upper story affords. Yet even within the upper level, the physical and immaterial merge. The partitions that define the rooms are also screens onto which videotapes, films, and digital art can be projected. "Our architectural treatment

of the space was devised to allow the exterior, the interior, and the artists' projected images to flow into each other," the architects remarked.

While clearly influenced by Ludwig Mies van der Rohe's Farnsworth House (fig. 7), the architects avoid facile references in the Kramlich Residence design. The modernist emphasis on clearly expressed and rationalized structure is suppressed, and the universal space so characteristic of Mies's work is replaced by a series of irregular, flowing volumes defined by undulating partitions. The overhanging roof, marked by skewed geometry and pierced by a rooftop terrace, is an autonomous architectural element. The terrace provides contact with the natural world, completing a vertical progression from what the architects have called the "virtual, mental space underground" to direct, physical experience.

Site plan

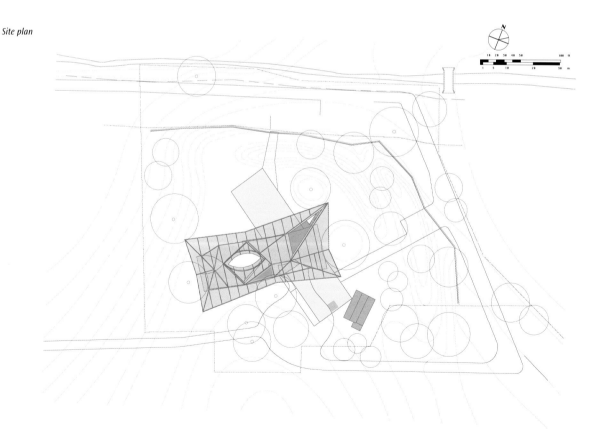

Lower-level interior with video installations: Steve McQueen's Just Above My Head *(1996) at left, Gary Hill's* Viewer *(1996) at back, and Jeff Wall's* The Quarrel *(1998) at right. Computer-generated image*

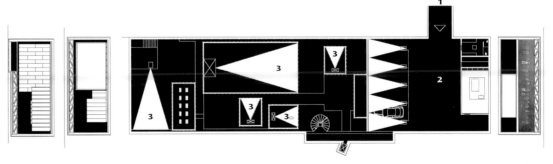

Longitudinal section along lower-level axis

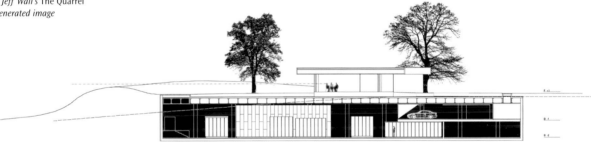

Three sections and lower-level plan
1 *Entry*
2 *Garage/video gallery*
3 *Video gallery*

Southeast elevation above with section through garage/video gallery below

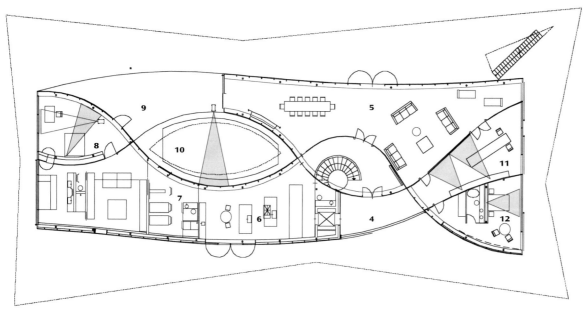

Ground-floor plan
  4 *Entry*
  5 *Living/dining area*
  6 *Kitchen*
  7 *Gym*
  8 *Master bedroom*
  9 *Terrace*
  10 *Pool*
  11 *Library*
  12 *Bedroom*

Ground-floor interior with Matthew Barney's Cremaster 4 *(1995–96) video installation at left. Computer-generated image with sketch*

Intended for a site sixty feet above Noyack Bay on North Haven Point on Long Island, New York, the Slow House was designed by Elizabeth Diller and Ricardo Scofidio for a young Japanese art collector and entrepreneur. Reflecting the shifting relationships between work and leisure in contemporary culture, the unbuilt Slow House might be described as a vacation/work space equipped to, in the words of the architects, "escape from escape, that is, to connect at a moment's notice back to the sites of anxiety."

In the design, two curving arcs frame the front door to the east and the picture window to the southwest. The height of the house increases from the single-story entrance to the two-story section in the rear, facing the view of the bay. The kitchen, dining, and living spaces are above, on the second floor, and the bedrooms below. As described by the architects, "The Slow House is conceived as an apparatus for producing a view. Simply, the house is a door that leads to a window, physical entry to optical departure."

The importance of the view, which Diller and Scofidio have called "the prized asset of the vacation home," is questioned by their planned placement of a video monitor in front of the picture window. A video camera would digitally duplicate the "natural" view of the water, allowing it to be played back whenever desired. In describing their juxtaposition of the real and the virtual, the architects state, "The two devices, the picture window and the video screen, share certain characteristics."

As the electronic view is mediated, so too is the view through the picture window. The cultural act of framing invests something with value. The picture window domesticates nature, collapsing its depth and turning it into a representation."

In a more subtle reference to its location, the house was designed to be built with a boatlike stressed-skin structure. A vertical framework is to be clad with two-by-four-inch structural lumber running horizontally, before being finished on the interior with plywood and on the exterior with horizontal planking.

Detail of TV in Picture Window Apparatus. Collage of exterior perspective, plans, color photocopies, pencil on Mylar (overlay), and green tape on board. The Museum of Modern Art, New York. Gift of the architects in honor of Lily Auchincloss

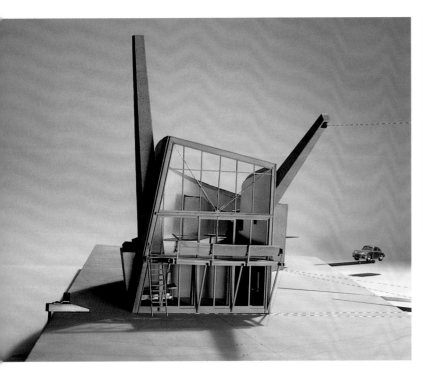

Above and facing page: Model. Wood, cardboard, metal, plastic, and twine. The Museum of Modern Art, New York. Marshall Cogan Purchase Fund, Bertha and Isaac Liberman Foundation Fund

Four exterior elevations, composite drawing

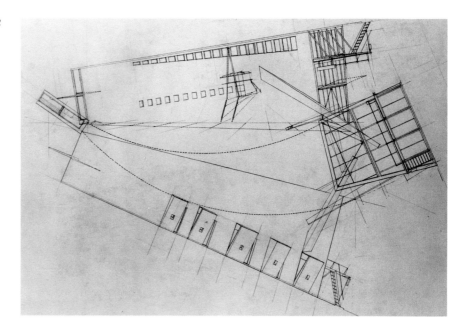

1 *Entry*
2 *Kitchen/dining area*
3 *Terrace*
4 *Living area*
5 *Bedroom*

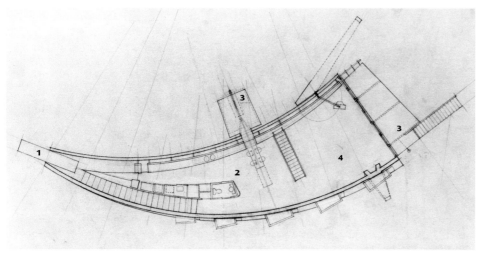

Keyed plan with transverse sections

Upper-level plan

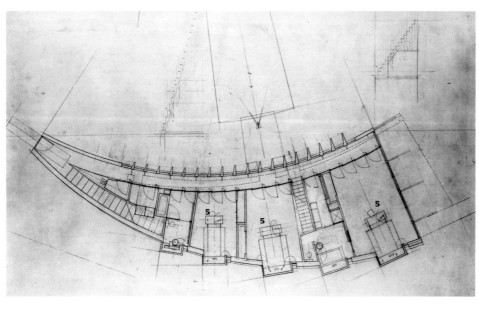

Ground-floor plan

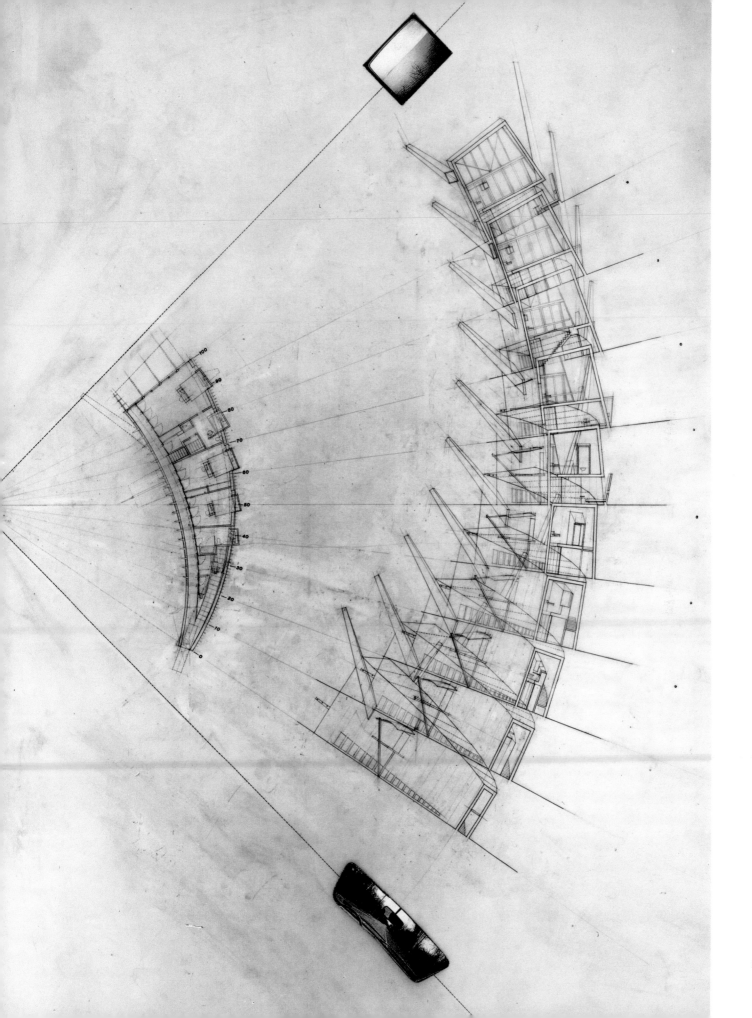

The Digital House was designed by Gisue Hariri and Mojgan Hariri for *House Beautiful* magazine to demonstrate the potential impact of new electronic technologies on the private house. The house design consists of a central structural core, built in situ, and factory-made "plug-in" volumes to serve various programmatic requirements for bedrooms, living areas, work spaces, and so on. These rooms, which would be delivered by truck, are considered more like appliances that can be added and exchanged to reflect new domestic situations.

The function of the central core would not simply be structural, however. The main walls would be made from liquid-crystal displays—what the architects call "the building blocks of the future"—

which are capable of collapsing the very notions of time and space. In the kitchen, for example, a virtual chef from a favorite restaurant could aid in the preparation of meals, and the residents could entertain friends who live thousands of miles away.

Connecting but in contrast to the house design's digital environments are its "transient spaces," which, the architects say, "allow the inhabitants to unplug themselves momentarily, as they move between tasks and from the virtual to the actual world. Here, the eye takes in a layering of realities as one can look into other parts of the house, to the landscape beyond, or to the images on the walls."

With this project, Hariri and Hariri do not simply imagine digital enhancements to existing domestic situations. Rather,

they investigate a conception of the house as an extension of the body, a "smart" environment that is not so much characterized by the presence of discrete computers but by surfaces and devices that are interactive. As a receiver and transmitter of information, the house also becomes an extension of the mind. The architects state, "In The Digital House, the comfort, safety, and stability of home can coexist with the risky possibilities of flight."

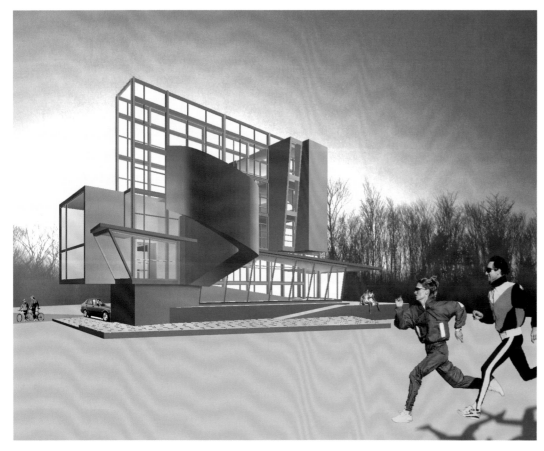

View of rear facade. Computer-generated image

Principal facade. Computer-generated image

View of principal facade. Computer-generated image

Kitchen with virtual chef. Computer-generated image

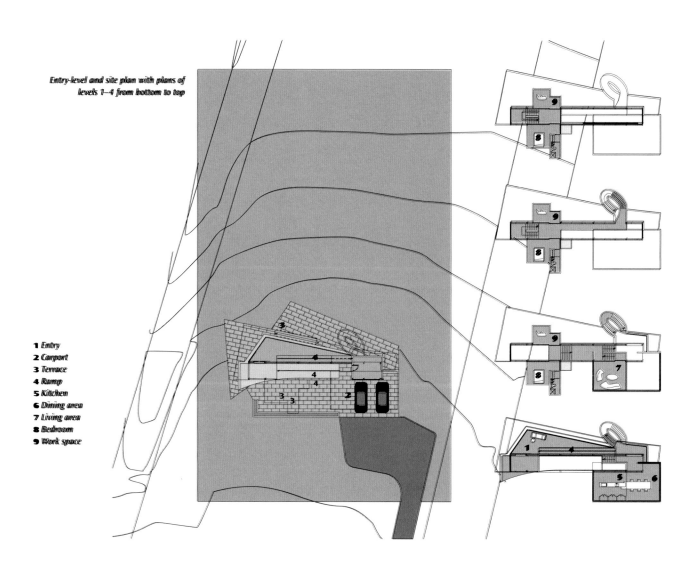

Entry-level and site plan with plans of
levels 1–4 from bottom to top

1 Entry
2 Carport
3 Terrace
4 Ramp
5 Kitchen
6 Dining area
7 Living area
8 Bedroom
9 Work space

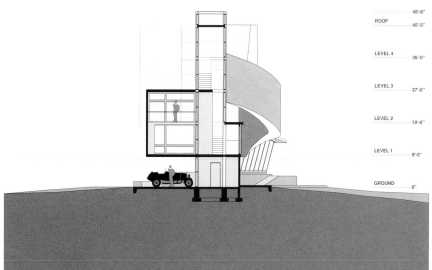

ROOF 48'-8"
45'-0"

LEVEL 4 36'-0"

LEVEL 3 27'-0"

LEVEL 2 18'-0"

LEVEL 1 9'-0"

GROUND 0"

Transverse section through living and dining areas

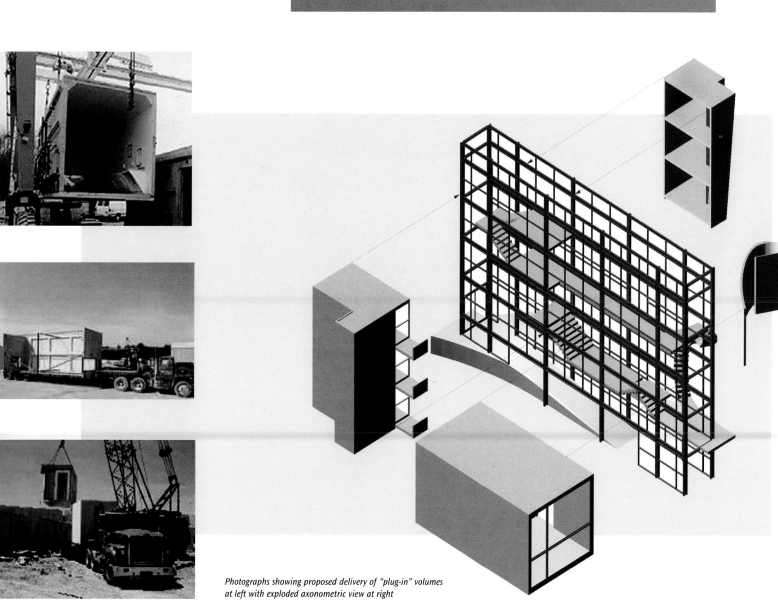

Photographs showing proposed delivery of "plug-in" volumes at left with exploded axonometric view at right

Borneo Sporenburg is a new housing district in Amsterdam; its master plan has been devised by Adriaan Geuze's West 8 Landscape Architects. To offset the high costs of land reclamation and site infrastructure, row houses were planned for the area to provide the most efficient housing in terms of space usage and overall cost. The houses now under construction on plots 12 and 18 were designed by a team from MVRDV comprised of Winy Maas, Jacob van Rijs, and Nathalie de Vries with Joost Glissenaar, Bart Spee, and Alex Brouwer. Arno van der Mark, artist, also contributed to the house on plot 12, and Frans de Witte to that on plot 18.

The house on plot 12, which measures 5 meters wide by 16 meters deep (about 16½ x 52½ feet), will serve as workplace and home for a couple: a sculptor and a creative-events consultant. The footprint of the main body of the house has been limited to half of the site's width, a mere 2.5 meters, leaving an equally wide slot of space as a semipublic "alley" that steps down from the level of the narrow street to that of the canal at the rear of the house. The unexpected strategy of the alley, which opens up the house to the street and to passersby, generates a row house that is seen not as a facade but as a volume, albeit a narrow one. In addition, the lateral facade is sheathed in glass, giving the house a high degree of transparency relative to its dense urban location. This openness reflects the interest of both the architects and clients in the spaces and events of the public realm.

The higher portion of the alley serves as a place to park a car as well as to greet arriving guests. The lower portion, facing the canal, is somewhat shielded from public scrutiny. Two opaque two-story volumes projecting out over the alley enliven the formal character of the interior and exterior spaces; one is to be an extension of the owners' work spaces on the second and third floors, and the other will contain a guest bedroom and bathroom.

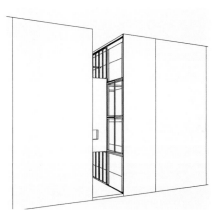

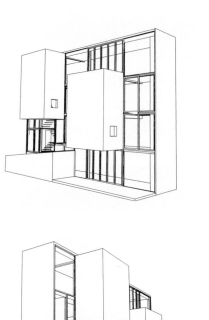

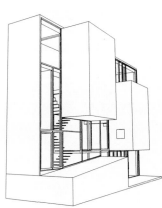

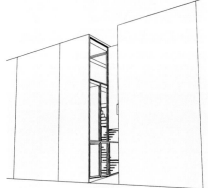

Borneo Sporenburg-12
Clockwise from top left: Section perspective from canal; perspective from canal with adjacent buildings; perspective from street with adjacent buildings; section perspective from street

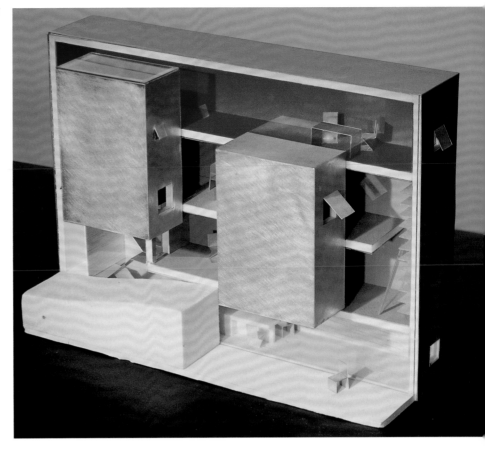

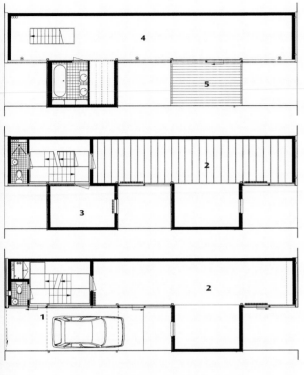

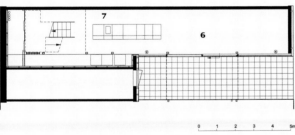

Borneo Sporenburg-12
From top to bottom: Fourth-floor, third-floor, entry-level
(second-floor), and lower-level plans

1 *Entry*
2 *Work space*
3 *Bedroom*
4 *Living area/bedroom*
5 *Terrace*
6 *Dining area*
7 *Kitchen*

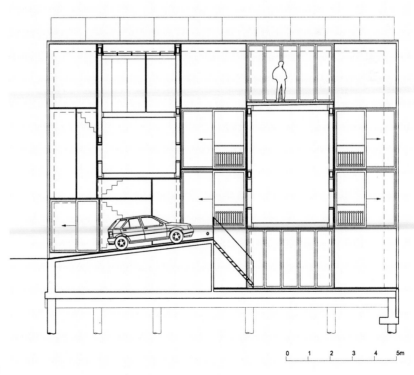

Borneo Sporenburg-12: Longitudinal
section through projecting volumes

Of all the houses planned for Borneo Sporenburg, the one on plot 18 will have the smallest interior square footage, as the master plan mandates that it include a garden within its small site. To compensate for the reduced interior dimensions, MVRDV conceived the house as one long, "continuous" room. The spaces of the house flow upward much like a vertical loft, encompassing loosely defined living, dining, and study areas. The fluid interior space connects with the outdoors at three junctures: the garden on the ground floor, an interior balcony on the second floor with a view toward the water, and a terrace on the roof over the bedroom.

The design guidelines might have suggested that the house follow the more or less traditional row-house pattern of higher spaces at ground level with two additional floors of slightly less height above. Through the architects' manipulations of the section, however, the house is more accurately described as having double-height spaces facing the street and canal, and compressed, almost cabinetlike rooms in the center for various programmatic functions. The high ceilings imbue the space with openness, a sensation enhanced by the glass facades on the street and canal sides. Like the house on plot 12, this building was conceived as more highly transparent and potentially open to public view than the great majority of row houses, which have traditionally adopted a more reclusive attitude in light of the implicit density of attached housing.

Borneo Sporenburg-18
Left: Perspective from canal through adjacent building
Right: Perspective from street through adjacent building

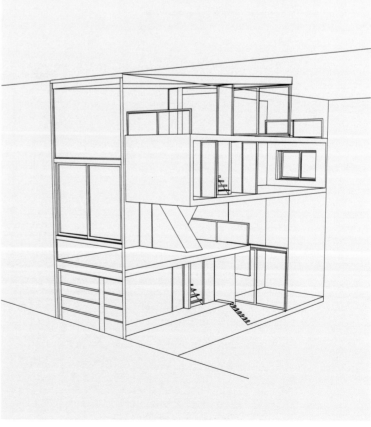

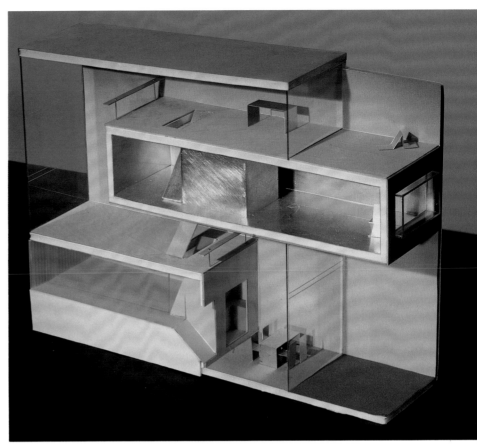

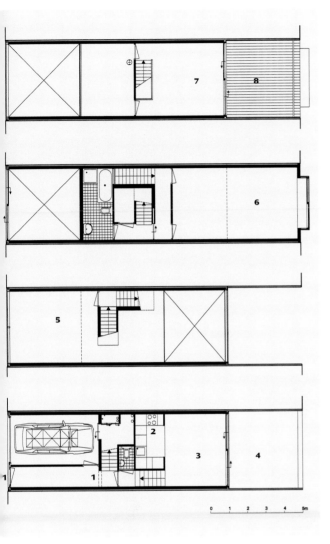

Borneo Sporenburg-18
From top to bottom: Fourth-floor, third-floor,
second-floor, and ground-floor plans

1 *Entry*
2 *Kitchen*
3 *Dining area*
4 *Garden*
5 *Living area*
6 *Bedroom*
7 *Work space*
8 *Terrace*

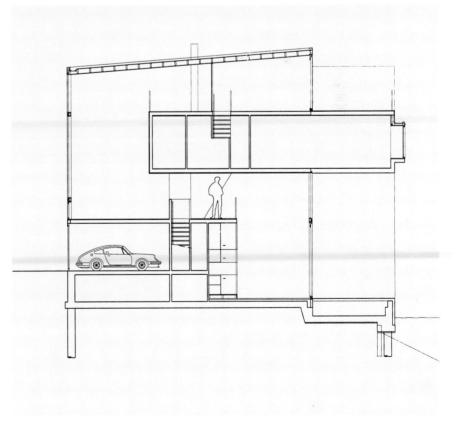

Borneo Sporenburg-18: Longitudinal section

Michael Bell's Glass House @ 2° was designed for a site in Houston's Fifth Ward, a neighborhood with a rich cultural heritage but stifled by the low incomes of its households. Conceived as a single-family house, the as-of-yet-unbuilt design meets the strict financial requirements of an experimental housing program of the federal government, wherein moneys previously available for multifamily buildings could be obtained as vouchers for the construction of private houses.

Slicing deep into the 900-square-foot house, long, narrow light wells nearly divide the structure into two and create a front section, with living and dining spaces, and a back section, for sleeping and bathing. The roof is a rigid, metal decking system, its strength derived from folds in the light-gauge metal.

That Bell designed a glass house for a low-income neighborhood intentionally underscores many of the ambiguities associated with this historically charged architectural type, which is typically identified with a certain level of sophisticated luxury. Bell, however, has proposed to construct his Glass House @ 2° of low-cost, standard, sliding glass door units. In citing the glass house's ability to reveal both its structure and the life of its inhabitants, the architect refers to glass's historically visionary qualities of transparency, openness, equality, and freedom. While he has acknowledged that glass may be seen to "desecrate" privacy, he also poses the question "Why should an invisible group of people choose to live behind walls rather than reveal their lives?"

As if to accentuate this unresolvable duality, Bell embedded a further contradiction within the form of the house itself. If Ludwig Mies van der Rohe's Farnsworth House (fig. 7) represented sophisticated luxury, it also embodied formal and technical refinement, if not perfection. The Glass House @ 2° derives its name from the building's slightly distorted shape, its rectilinear volume and now tensed midsection appearing to have been wracked by some external pressure.

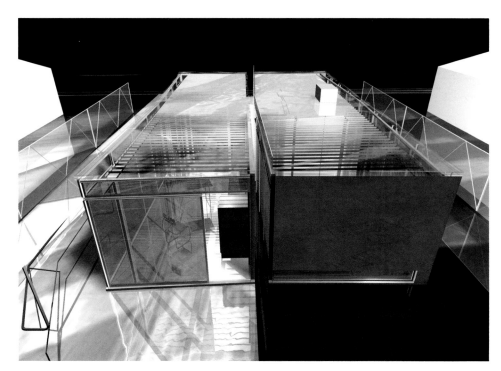

View of rear facade. Computer-generated image

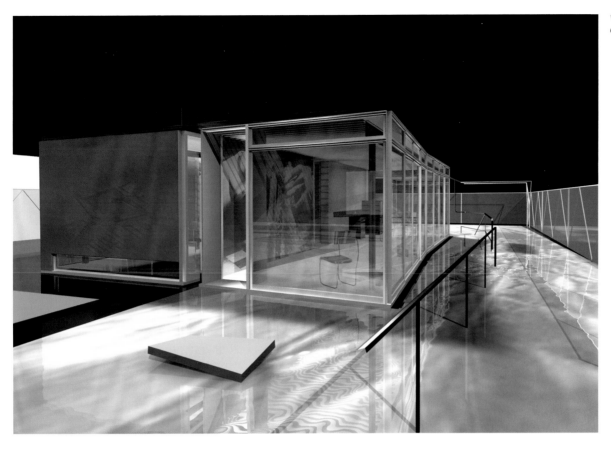

View of entry facade. Computer-generated image

View into bedroom on left and entry and living area on right. Computer-generated image

Aerial view from northeast with roof rendered transparent. Computer-generated image

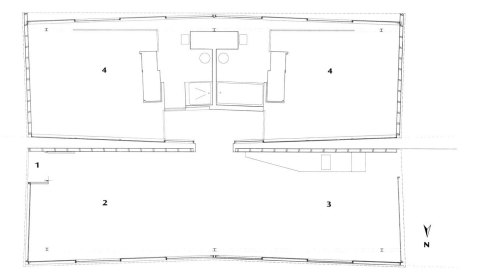

Plan
1 Entry
2 Living area
3 Kitchen/dining area
4 Bedroom

N

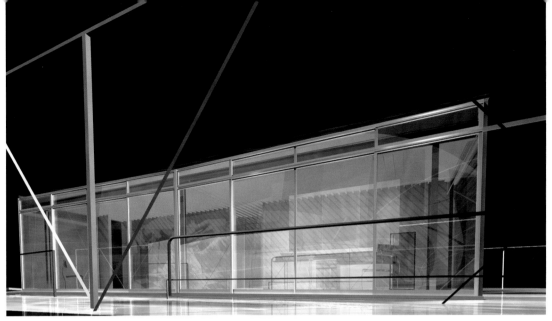

View into kitchen/dining and living areas from northwest. Computer-generated image

View into bedroom from southeast. Computer-generated image

Bernard Tschumi designed The Hague Villa, an unbuilt house with four bedrooms and two adjoining studios, for a site between a canal and a major roadway in an area newly under development in the Dutch capital. Conceived to be a living and working environment, the design is a dynamically unstable composition, constituting a somewhat fractious dialogue between opposites: the permanent, solid, and material versus the fleeting, transparent, and immaterial. The principal living and working spaces are found in a three-story glass volume. The bedrooms, that is, the intimate spaces, are enclosed within the opaque, concrete volume that hovers over the ground floor, which is comprised of the kitchen and storage areas. The bathroom core, according to Tschumi, acts as a "crankshaft" that "locks the other elements in place." The tilt of the glass volume away from the rest of the structure suggests a shift away from the privacy of the household realm in favor of a more public expression.

The architect's use of the free plan, roof terrace, and other imagery influenced by Le Corbusier's language invokes the modern master's precept of the house as a "machine for living in." However, that high-modernist conception of the mechanized domicile is countered by the contemporary image of the house as interactive device, suggesting the increasingly complex relationships between the public and private worlds. Thus, the architect not only associates his glass volume with the idea of visual permeability but also with the extent to which houses have become receivers and transmitters of electronic data: "The appearance of permanence (i.e., buildings are solid; they are made of steel, concrete, bricks, etc.) is increasingly challenged by the immaterial representation of abstract systems (television and electronic images).... The borders of The Hague Villa's living room and work space, devoid of the camouflage of ornament, expand beyond the property lines just as they are undermined by the electronic devices of everyday use that they contain."

Model

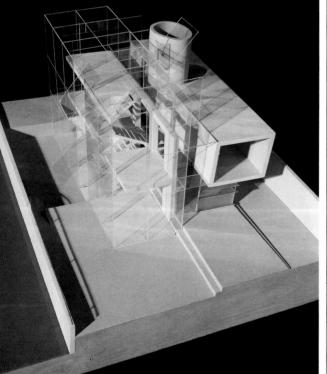

Perspective from east

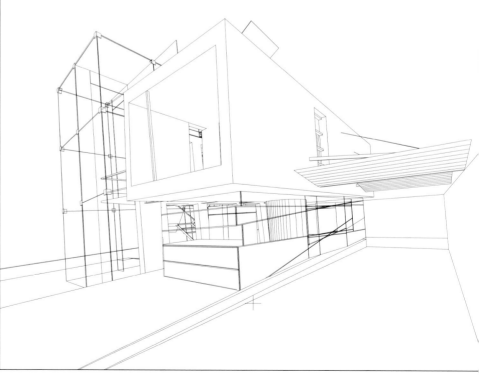

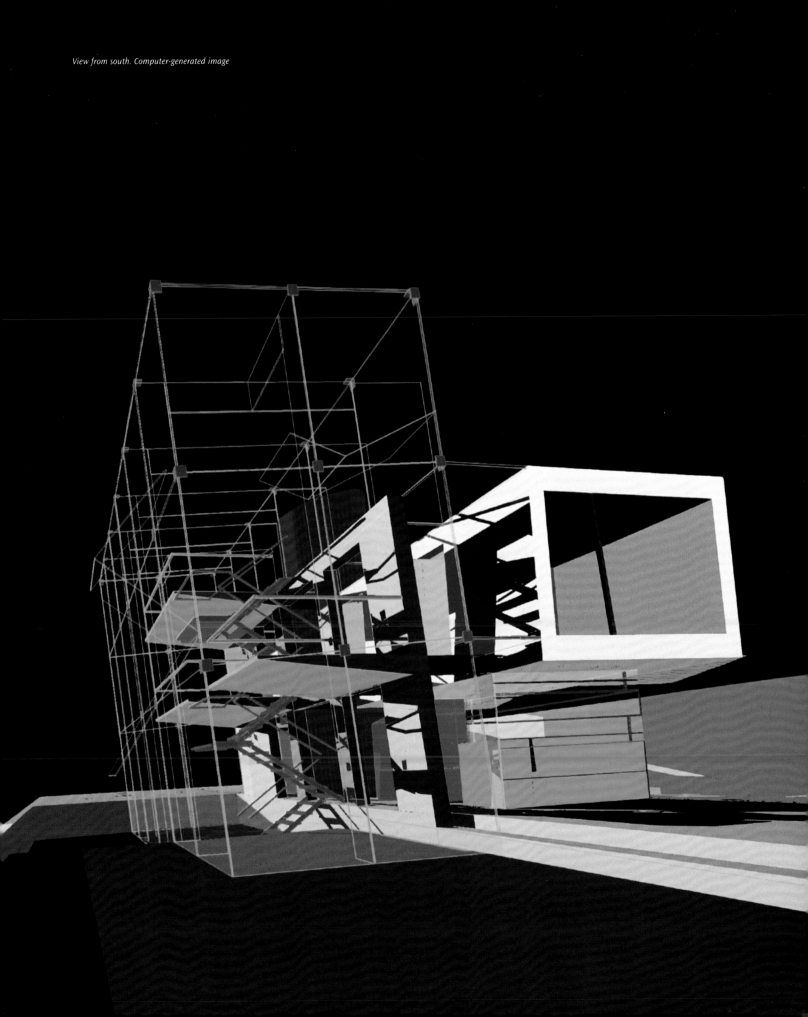

View from south. Computer-generated image

Aerial perspective from north

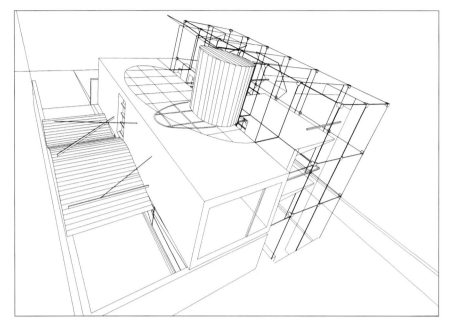

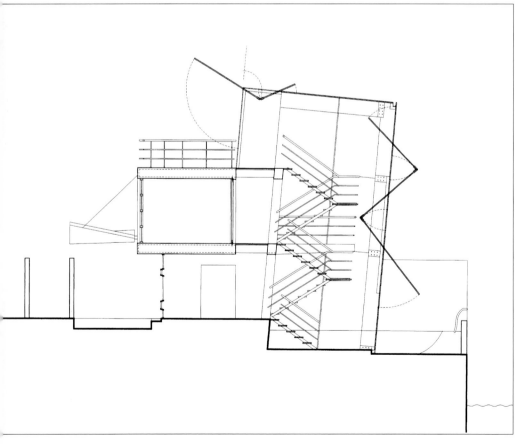

Transverse section

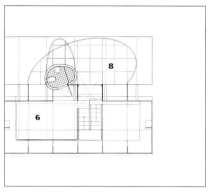

Third-floor plan

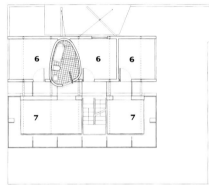

Second-floor plan

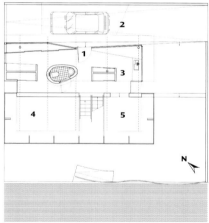

Ground-floor plan

1 *Entry*
2 *Carport*
3 *Kitchen*
4 *Living area*
5 *Dining area*
6 *Bedroom*
7 *Work space*
8 *Terrace*

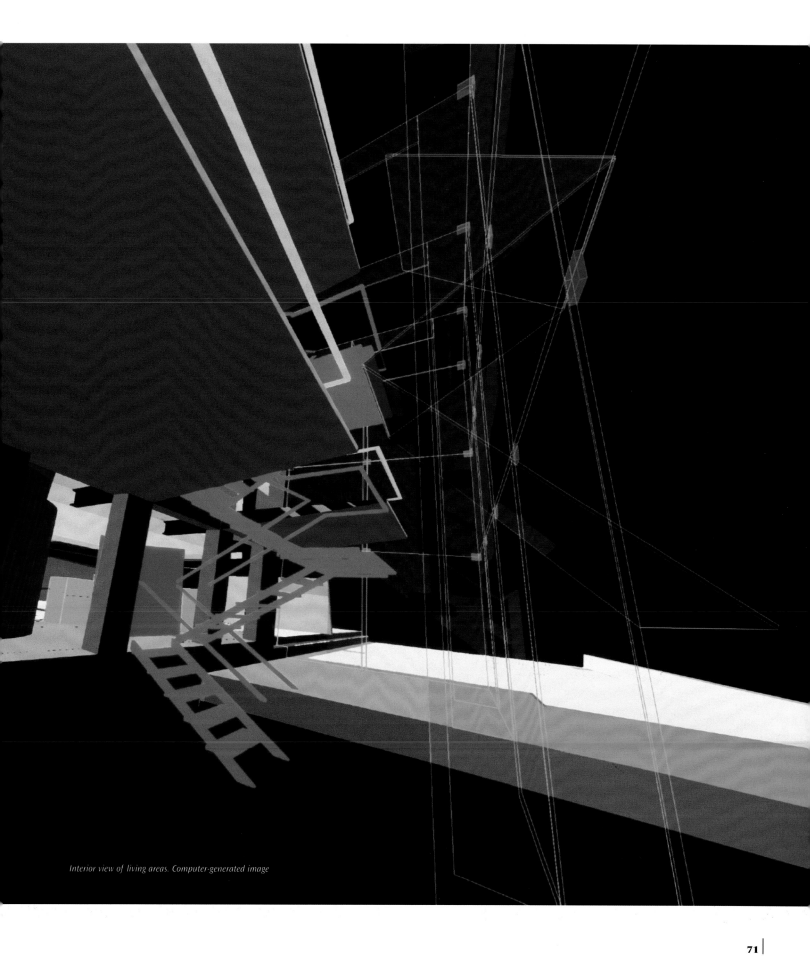

Interior view of living areas. Computer-generated image

The three-story Curtain Wall House was designed by Shigeru Ban for a family in Itabashi, a dense residential neighborhood in Tokyo. The project comprised the complete redesign and transformation of a preexisting Japanese-style residence to satisfy the clients' wish to live in a house that is not only constructed of contemporary materials but also evinces the openness and freedom associated with contemporary life.

The degree of privacy and the quality of the interior spaces, not unlike those in a traditional Japanese home, can be manipulated. Instead of the lightweight partitions in a traditional house, a dramatic fabric curtain spans the second and third floors. "This thin membrane takes the place of *shoji* screens, *fusuma* doors, shutters, and *sudare* screens in the traditional Japanese house," according to Ban. The curtain—as well as the house's glazed facades—can be opened and closed to alter the view and environmental effects such as light and wind. When the curtain is closed at night, the house appears to glow from within; when it is fully opened during the day, the occupants appear, as much as anything else, to be living on the decks of a ship.

Raised up on columns to allow automobiles to park on ground level, the second floor contains the principal shared spaces—living and dining areas and kitchen. Separated from the shared spaces are the three bedrooms on the third level. A terrace wraps around the second floor and extends its spaces out into the city itself. Contrasting with the openness of the living areas and even the bedrooms, the various functional spaces—a studio, stairs, and bathrooms—are contained in more organically shaped volumes at the rear of the structure.

Aside from its punning on the notion of the "curtain wall" (a non-load-bearing exterior wall), Ban's design recalls residential structures of the past, like tents, huts, and yurts, that are enclosures made of fibers or other natural materials. Equally, the project displays a taste for the surreal, while maintaining its connections to local construction techniques.

Exploded axonometric view

View with curtains closed

Right: View with curtains open

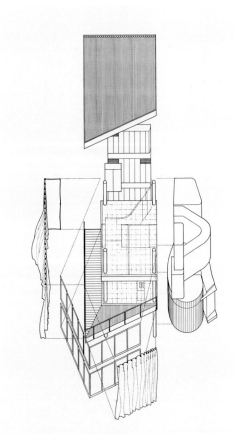

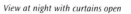
View at night with curtains open

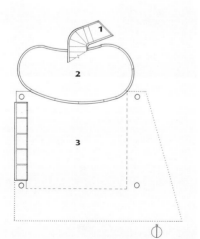

Dining area and terrace

1 *Entry*
2 *Work space*
3 *Garage*
4 *Living/dining area*
5 *Kitchen*
6 *Terrace*
7 *Bedroom*

Ground-floor plan

Second-floor plan

Third-floor plan

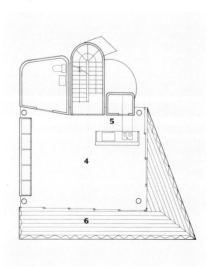

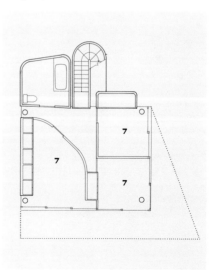

The Hergott Shepard Residence was designed by Michael Maltzan for a gay couple, both professionals in the entertainment industry. The house occupies nearly all of the usable area of a site that drops off steeply in the rear, offering spectacular views of Los Angeles. With its length running parallel to the street, the house is a carefully calculated rectilinear composition held together by two diagonally related volumes, which are clad in distinctive zinc panels and contain the main living areas. Running between the two volumes is a longitudinal axis that interweaves these spaces with the gymnasium and dining area on the ground level and the office and bedroom above.

As in Ludwig Mies van der Rohe's Tugendhat House (Brno, Czech Republic, 1928–30), the path through the house is complex, moving back and forth along the site rather than directly across it. The visitor approaches the entrance by traversing the length of the house along a low wall. Upon entering, one senses that the space is momentarily contained within the two central volumes, in which the owners' extensive collection of contemporary art is on display, before drifting laterally through the house. Dramatic views are revealed to the visitor in a measured fashion. Passing through the house to the rear yard, the viewer is again guided—in this case by a retaining wall—along the length of the site, which overlooks the city below.

From the street side, the house is composed of a series of large volumes that do not offer any direct views into the interior. However, on the rear of the house, the scale is reduced and the solidity of the front gives way to transparency. The sense of privacy this arrangement affords has a counterpoint in the interrelated interior spaces, which the clients, who entertain for both business and political causes, conceived as having a public dimension.

In its overall pragmatism, its sensual response to the landscape, and its skillful interpretations of modern design principles, the Hergott Shepard Residence reflects the ongoing influence of the architecture of Southern California, a crucible for contemporary culture.

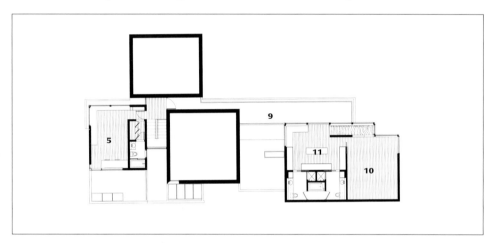

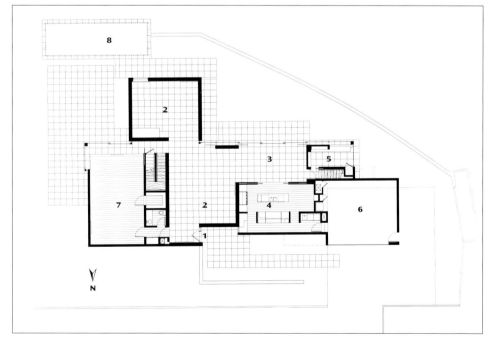

Top: Upper-level plan
Bottom: Ground-floor plan

1 *Entry*
2 *Living area*
3 *Dining area*
4 *Kitchen*
5 *Work space*
6 *Garage*
7 *Gym*
8 *Pool*
9 *Terrace*
10 *Master bedroom*
11 *Dressing area*

Principal facade

South elevation

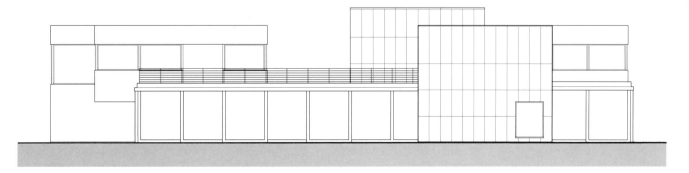

*Clockwise from top left: View of terrace from dressing area;
view of stairs from master bedroom with terrace at right; view
into gym from south; living areas*

View into dining area from south

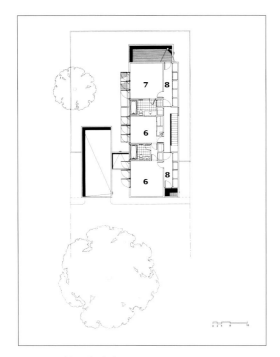

Upper-level plan

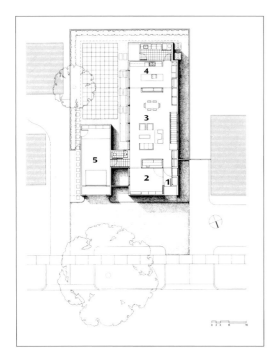

Ground-floor plan

1 *Entry*
2 *Work space*
3 *Living/dining area*
4 *Kitchen*
5 *Garage*
6 *Bedroom*
7 *Master bedroom*
8 *Dressing room/corridor*

Designed by Francois de Menil for a single woman, the 3,480-square-foot, white stucco Shorthand House was constructed in 1996–97 on a site in a relatively dense Houston neighborhood. Anticipating the day she would no longer be working full-time, the client chose the site because it would allow her to walk more and drive less as she went about her daily routines.

The house is composed of a two-story volume, which runs the length of the lot, and a single-story garage. A blind passage connects the two, giving the entry facade a discreetly composed presence and creating an L-shaped plan that screens a landscaped courtyard from the main street. Bedrooms on the upper level of the house accommodate the owner and her friends or her adult children who might be visiting. In both the bedrooms and the living areas below, the few window openings facing the street or the neighbors are balanced by the continuous glazing facing the light-filled landscaped courtyard.

In describing the name given to the project, the architect has said, "The Shorthand House seeks to introduce basic spatial awareness and potentiality to the suburban domestic environment by translating the linguistic rules of shorthand [a system in which the client was well versed] into a flexible system of symbolic architectural references." In one sense, de Menil's efficient, architectural shorthand is achieved by using an essential element rather than walls to express the function of a room: a table defines the dining room; a hearth defines the living room. In addition, a series of moving partitions and doors, mimicking the gestural characters of shorthand, transforms the open spaces of the house for different functions. An open sitting area, for example, quickly becomes an enclosed work space; a hallway becomes a dressing room. Thus, the apparent boundaries of each room are flexible, and the owner can adapt the architecture to her current needs. The architect concludes, "Because the occupant must physically engage the house in order to alter the spatial condition, she is, of necessity, simultaneously engaged in understanding the meaning and experience of space and architecture."

Principal facade

View into interior from courtyard

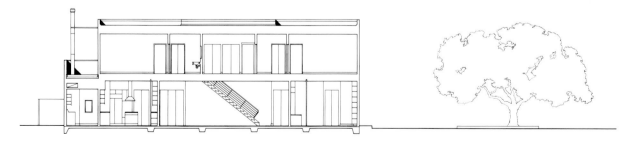

Longitudinal section

View into bedroom (above) and work space (below) from court

Work space with movable panels retracted

Plan of work space with movable panels retracted

Work space with movable panels extended

Plan of work space with movable panels extended

64 Wakefield as it now appears is the most recent design by Mack Scogin and Merrill Elam for their own house on a plot in an Atlanta neighborhood of bungalow-type houses. In the 1970s, they had renovated and opened up their bungalow, before adding two small freestanding structures in the rear for Scogin's son and guests. While these smaller structures survive as a guest pavilion, the bungalow was nearly destroyed by a hurricane in 1995.

About planning the new house for the same site, the architects have said, "The idea of a lap pool drove the process: dreams of exercise and relaxation, recollections of the Josephine Baker House, visions of the Italian rationalists' health clinics." Only the compact site's seventy-foot width offered the requisite space for the pool. Their solution was to suspend it at the house's upper level, spanning the living spaces of the floor below and taking advantage of the southern exposure. "Shielded from the street by a translucent glass wall but open to the sky and air, the roof deck and pool challenge the very notion of public/private. Materials mutate from translucent to opaque, from trans-

parent to reflective, and the house flickers between exposure and introversion," Scogin and Elam have remarked.

Unlike most houses in the neighborhood, the ambiguity between public and private is evident in the building's main elevation as well. Large expanses of glass reveal the spaces within, unscreened by conventional transitional spaces such as vestibules and entrance halls. Unlike the bungalow that preceded it, the current house is characterized by open, flowing spaces without fixed functions. Furthermore, the spatial organization is not limited to the horizontal dimension. The master suite is arranged vertically, challenging the traditional domestic hierarchy of upstairs/downstairs and private/public.

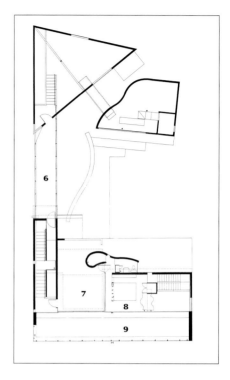

Top: Upper-level plan
Bottom: Ground-floor plan

1 *Entry*
2 *Living area*
3 *Dressing room*
4 *Carport*
5 *Guest pavilion*
6 *Library*
7 *Terrace*
8 *Master bedroom*
9 *Lap pool*

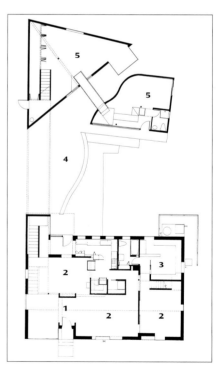

Principal facade

View into master bedroom from lap pool

Living areas

The BV House, designed by Homa Farjadi and Sima Farjadi, is sited on a hill overlooking the Ribble Valley. To be completed in 1999, it will serve as home and workplace for a couple and their three children. In its siting, its extensive architectonic terraces and gardens, and its topographical response, the house hovers between architecture and landscape design. The architects have said that "the house is a mass formed of striated layers of space. Ordinary spaces and habits in the house and the landscape are given new conditions."

The house was conceived as three distinct components: the shared social areas; the parents' spaces, among them a bedroom suite and offices; and the children's wing. The insertion of exterior space between the major programmatic elements both connects and distances the inhabitants of the house. A lily pond, traversed by two bridges, lies between the common spaces and the parents' suite; the children's "house" is freestanding but physically connected to the principal structure by a canopied area.

The somewhat ambiguous programmatic organization is mirrored on the interior. Walls have sliding segments that divide and connect contiguous living spaces and provide variable openings. Movable partitions also promote a shifting sense of privacy. For example, the wall of the master bath can be slid away, creating a direct visual and physical connection to the lily pond.

As if to critique the pale references in many contemporary English houses to the domestic architecture of C. F. A. Voysey, an Arts and Crafts designer, the BV House eschews the traditional peaked roof for a "creased" roof, which Farjadi and Farjadi have compared to an "undulating deck." In a further repositioning of traditional building practices, the vertical surfaces of the house are clad in thatch, typically a roofing material, which gives the structures a highly tactile quality as well as additional insulation and protection from the rain.

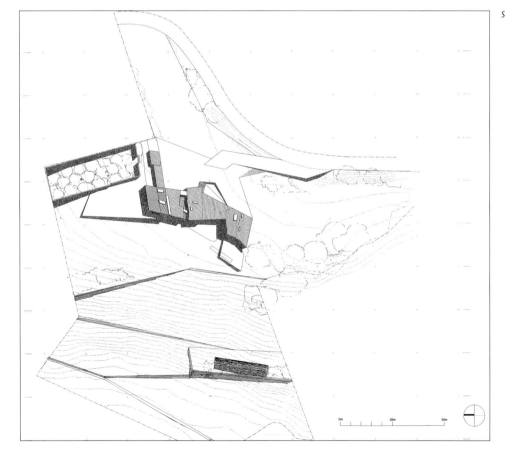

Site plan

Hillside view from northwest. Computer-generated image

1 Entry
2 Living area
3 Dining area
4 Lily pond
5 Work space
6 Master bedroom
7 Bedroom
8 Covered passage
9 Pool room
10 Jacuzzi/sauna

Lower-level plan

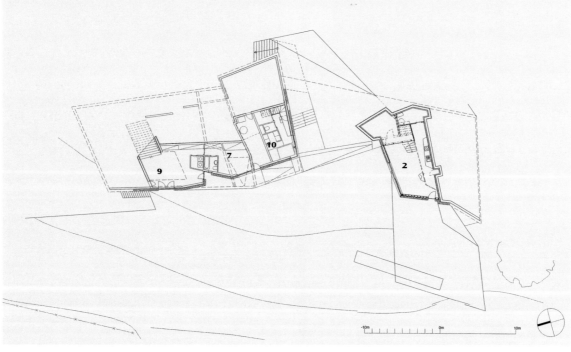

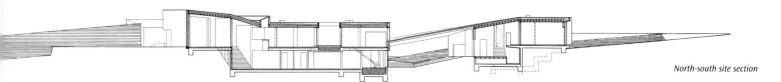

North-south site section

Dining area from lily pond. Computer-generated image

Lily pond between dining area and master bedroom.
Computer-generated image

Sited on a hilltop with dramatic views over Bordeaux, this house was designed for a couple and their three children by Rem Koolhaas. The commission for Maison à Bordeaux reflected the physical and, more importantly, psychological needs of the husband, who, following an automobile accident, uses a wheelchair. "Contrary to what you would expect, I do not want a simple house. I want a complex house, because the house will define my world," he said.

In plan, a spiraling ramp provides entry from the road below to a courtyard, which is bounded by service spaces and guest facilities to the northeast and by the house itself to the southwest. In section, the house exhibits the same schema of a central void bounded by two volumes. The architect's basic conception of the project was as three "houses" on top of one another. The spaces devoted to family life, such as the kitchen and dining area, are on the lower level, half excavated from the earth. The more private, individual spaces for the parents and children (bedrooms and bathrooms) are on the top level, framed in cast concrete. Of the central void, Koolhaas has said: "The most important house was almost invisible, sand-wiched in between: a glass room—half inside, half outside—for living."

The horizontal striation in the "three houses" is echoed in the three stairways. Two of them lead, independently, from the lower level through the middle-level to the children's and parents' sections above; a third, "formal," staircase takes visitors from the lower to the middle level. In addition, a very large lift open on all sides travels between the three levels. Like an itinerant room, it moves alongside a three-story wall of shelves holding books, files, artworks, and wine within the husband's easy reach. In the words of the architect: "The movement of the elevator continuously changes the architecture of the house. A machine is its heart."

View of middle-level living area from terrace

1 *Entry*
2 *Kitchen/dining area*
3 *Elevator room*
4 *Family room*
5 *Entry ramp*
6 *Caretaker's house*
7 *Guest house*
8 *Living area*
9 *Work space*
10 *Terrace*
11 *Wife's bedroom*
12 *Husband's bedroom*
13 *Bedroom*

Lower-level plan

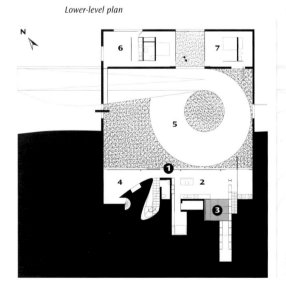

Middle-level plan

Upper-level plan

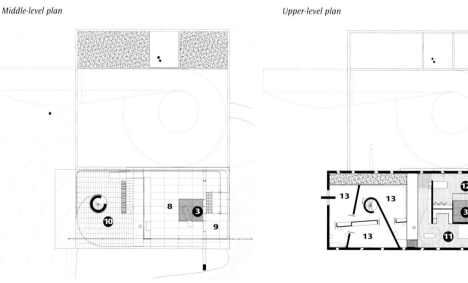

View from southwest

View from west

View of principal facade, courtyard, and entry ramp from east

93

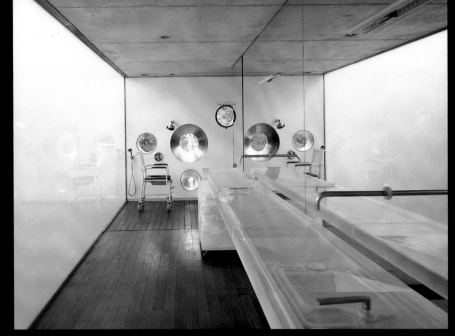

Master bathroom

Children's bedroom

Kitchen

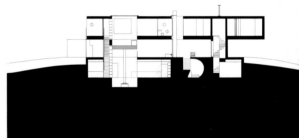

Longitudinal section

Top to bottom: Views of middle level with elevator room, with elevator room descended, and with guardrail in place

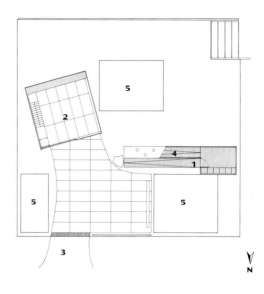

View of roof court with garage at left and entry ramp at right

Roof plan
1 *Entry*
2 *Garage*
3 *Driveway*
4 *Entry ramp*
5 *Courtyard*

Designed for a couple and their teenage children by Xaveer de Geyter, the House in Brasschaat is located in a suburban enclave of sandy dunes and scrub pines outside Antwerp. The house itself is sited such that it is scarcely recognizable from the street. The driveway ascends a dune to a paved court, which is the roof of the house, and leads to the garage, a free-standing glass cube that is skewed at an angle and resembles an enormous lantern. From the court, an external ramp leads down half a level to the house's main entrance. Inside, the ramp then switches back, running down another half level to the living spaces. At the base of the ramp, the visitor is led along a diagonal axis—parallel to the plan of the garage above—through the entrance hall and toward the main living spaces and the formal gardens beyond.

Separate "apartments" are included for the parents (on the west) and the children (on the north), each with sleeping and bathing rooms. Additionally, both of the parents have offices that allow them to work at home. Three courtyards are cut into the house's rectangular plan. The largest of these provides a sheltered space adjacent to living areas; the smaller ones, along with a glass-enclosed winter garden, provide varied and unexpected sources of light as well as more intimate spaces related to the "apartments."

Designed by Yves Brunier, the formal gardens reflect the sophisticated formal transformations of the high modernist vocabulary that defines the house. A trace of Le Corbusier's Villa Savoye (Poissy, France, 1929–31) can be seen in the switchback ramp; a Miesian steel and glass "arcade" faces the formal garden. While retaining the sense of comfort and casual living that, in the best cases, suburban living offers, the house avoids any concession to preconceived notions of domesticity and its associated imagery.

Aerial view. Mixed-media collage

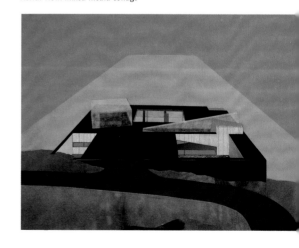

View from south

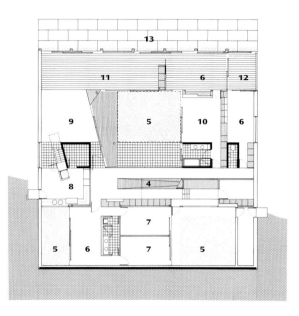

Plan
  4 Entry ramp
  5 Courtyard
  6 Work space
  7 Bedroom
  8 Kitchen
  9 Dining area
  10 Master bedroom
  11 Living area
  12 Winter garden
  13 Terrace

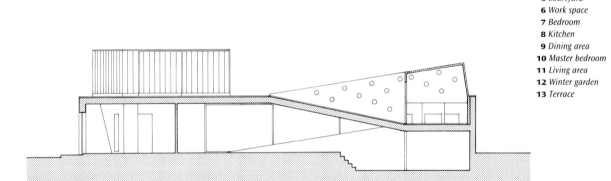

Section through entry ramp

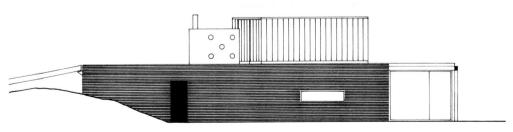

West elevation

View of entry ramp and partial view of central courtyard from roof

Entry

View of central courtyard toward formal gardens

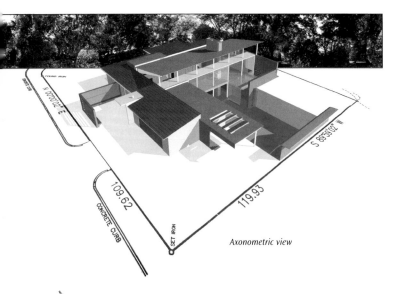

Axonometric view

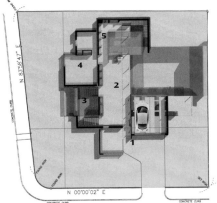

Entry-level (ground-floor) and site plan
1 *Entry*
2 *Kitchen/dining/living area*
3 *Study*
4 *Bedroom*
5 *Dressing room*

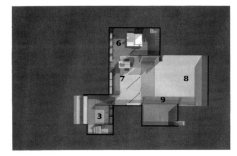

Lower-level plan
6 *Master bedroom*
7 *Master bathroom*
8 *Exercise area*
9 *Lap pool*

In the House for a Bachelor, an extensive renovation of a 1950s house in Minneapolis, Joel Sanders rethinks the American suburban single-family residence, adapting it to meet the domestic requirements of a single professional man. The unrealized design broadly addresses, in often witty and sometimes ironic ways, the many issues faced by men and women who choose to live alone or in relationships that are not defined by marriage and raising children.

Inspired in part by 1950s "bachelor pads" popularized in the postwar press, the program includes a reconfiguration and expansion of the single-room/single-function scheme of the original house. The renovation provides a more open kitchen/dining/living area, a two-level master-bedroom suite with a similar open flow of spaces, and a den that doubles as a home office.

To avoid having to obtain a variance to build a second floor, the site is to be excavated to create a subterranean backyard. Out of the neighbors' view, it is com-

prised of an Astroturf exercise area that flows spatially into the master bath, conceived as an "underground spa," and the rest of the master suite. Retaining its original street facades, the house assumes a dynamic character on the interior, which is atypical of the single-story developer houses surrounding it.

The House for a Bachelor is, in the words of Sanders, "based on the premise that nature (the landscape) and human identity are primarily social constructs. The surfaces that clothe the building—glass, wood paneling, mirror, television screens, and Astroturf, etc.—work like clothing that wraps the body, helping the bachelor to fabricate identity." The complex realization of this concept can be seen throughout the design. For example, in order to select his attire, the bachelor can hang his clothes on pegs on a dressing screen that is opposite a wall of closets. Made of semitransparent mirrored panels, this screen is a window wall that enables the bachelor to simultaneously observe the manicured backyard

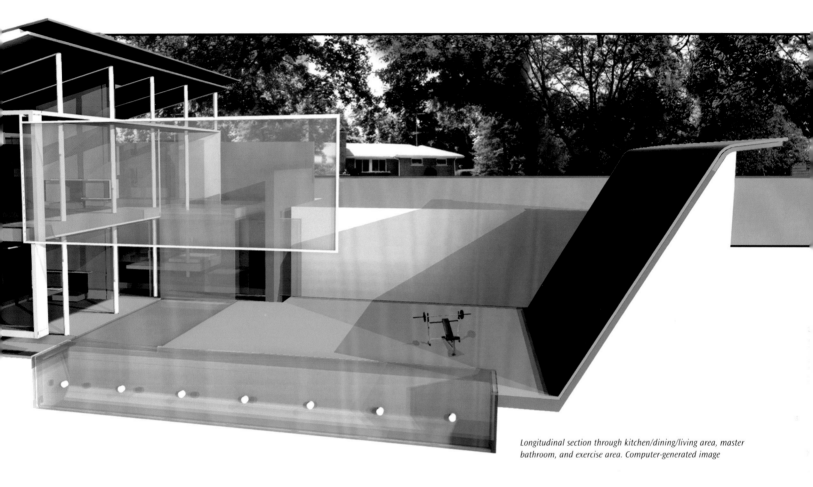

Longitudinal section through kitchen/dining/living area, master bathroom, and exercise area. Computer-generated image

and himself while dressing. In the den/study, a tropical-plant-filled terrarium replacing an existing window adjoins a projection television screen, merging them into, according to the architect, a new kind of window. Seen from an Eames lounge chair, an archetypal object of postwar interiors, the ensemble becomes a commentary on the cultural frames of both the picture window and the television, offering views onto the American suburban landscape and its media representations.

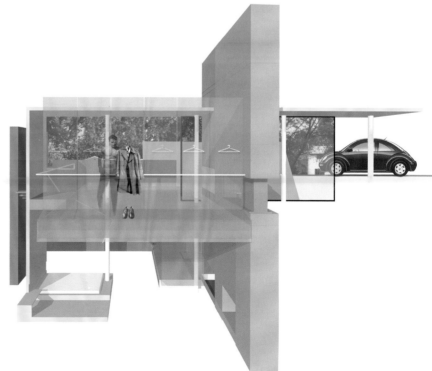

Transverse section through dressing area (above) and master bedroom (below). Computer-generated image

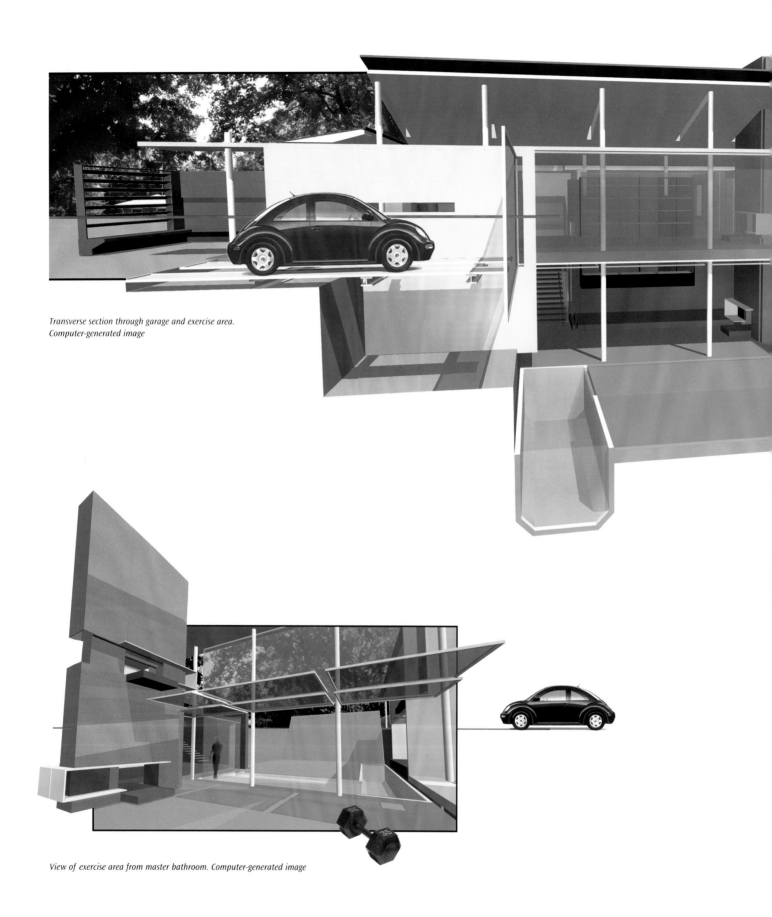

*Transverse section through garage and exercise area.
Computer-generated image*

View of exercise area from master bathroom. Computer-generated image

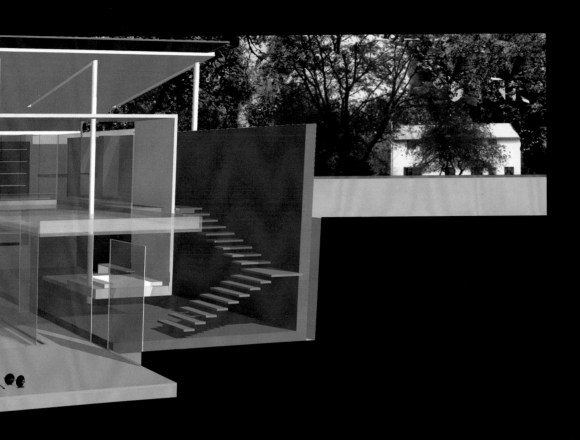

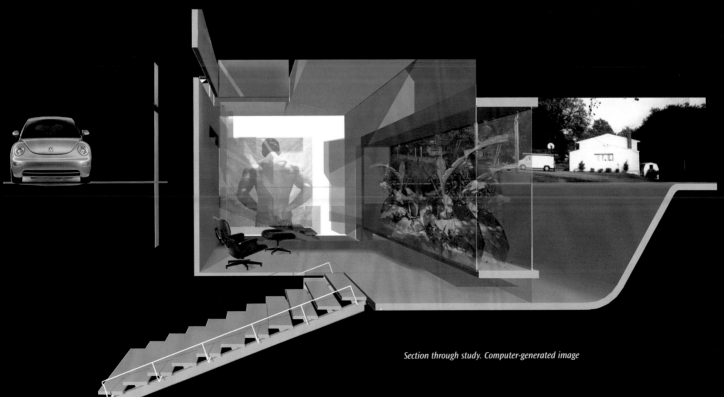

Section through study. Computer-generated image

The Torus House, designed by Preston Scott Cohen, represents a contemporary revision of the artist's house, a type of residence rooted in the nineteenth-century Arts and Crafts movement. The two largest spaces in the house will be painting studios. One is to be used for preparing large canvases. The other is for easel painting and will also serve as a gallery and a living space. Adjacent to these larger spaces will be more compact areas, including kitchen, office, bedrooms, and bathrooms, arranged to yield the maximum square footage to the two studios. The architect has noted the "centrifugal" effect of his organization, with the smaller spaces on the building's perimeter.

The approach to the house is to be from the lower end of the site, a gently sloping, partially wooded field. After parking under the easel-painting studio, the visitor will ascend a ramped foyer that leads into the house and also connects the two studios. Spatially and visually, the vertical circulation links all the principal elements of the house.

The formal character of the Torus House design is remarkable for its melding of seemingly incompatible geometric languages. The architect hopes to reinvigorate the historical tension between the orthodox and the radical: "The dialectic between norm and exception in architecture relies on the persistence or memory of social and building conventions on the one hand and formal transgression on the other." In this instance, the norm is a courtyard house, which is transformed by the use of nonarchitectural, seamless, curvilinear forms derived from the torus. That topological form is generated by rotating one circle along the path of a second, larger circle, usually producing a doughnutlike shape.

Amplifying the ambiguity between the house's interior and exterior, a stair, which occupies what would be the hollow core of the torus, bypasses the interior of the house by running directly from parking below to the roof above. Says Cohen, "The curvilinear lines and undulations blend the individual components into an unbroken surface that resembles features of the landscape beyond."

View into easel-painting studio from terrace. Computer-generated image

Site plan

Model

View of easel-painting studio and living area. Computer-generated image

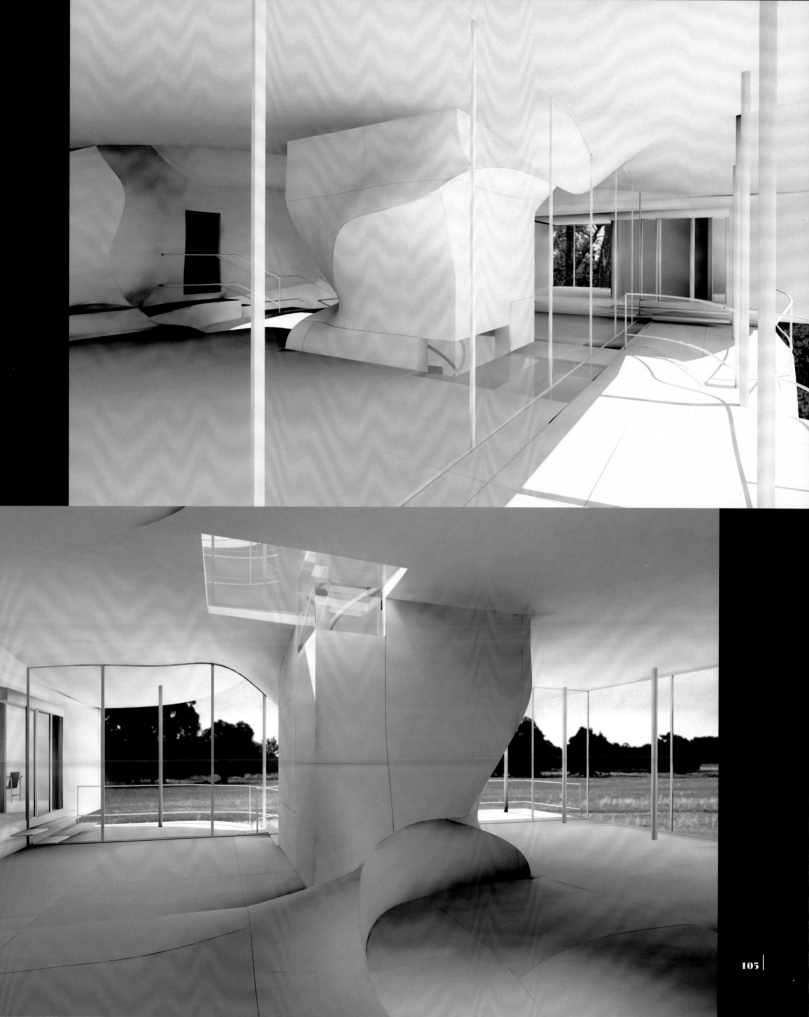

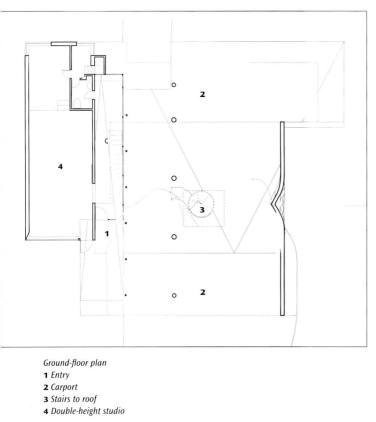

Ground-floor plan
1 Entry
2 Carport
3 Stairs to roof
4 Double-height studio

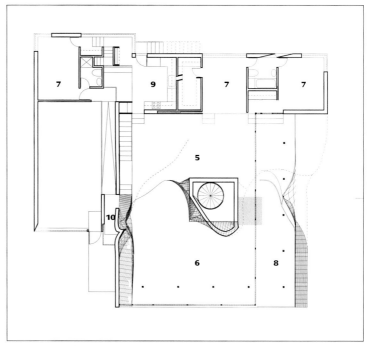

Upper-level plan
5 Living area
6 Easel-painting studio
7 Bedroom
8 Terrace
9 Kitchen
10 Office

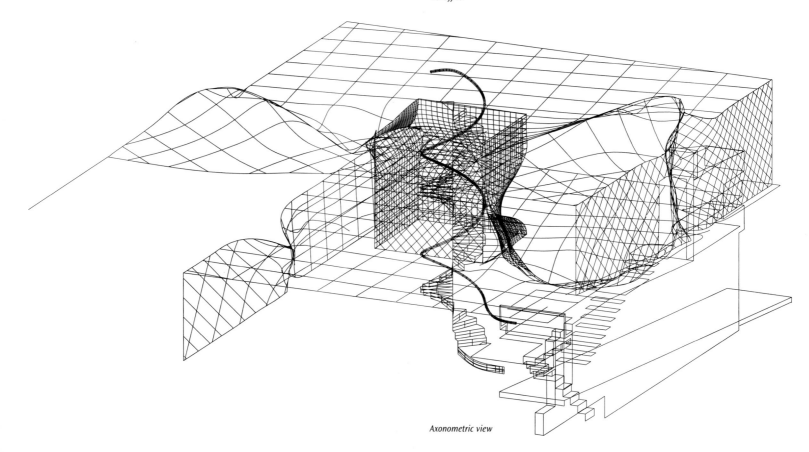

Axonometric view

View of ramp landing where it becomes kitchen table.
Computer-generated image

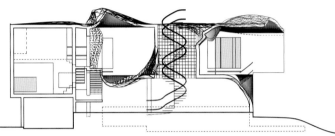

East-west section

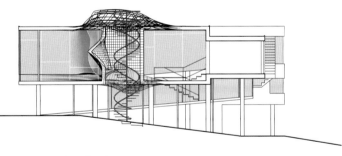

North-south section

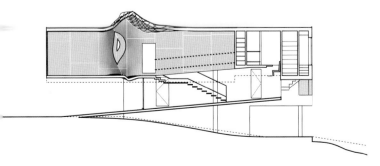

North-south section

Simon Ungers and Thomas Kinslow designed the T-House for a twenty-six-year-old single man, a writer by profession. Located on a rural site in upstate New York, the 2,500-square-foot house is both a residence and a library for ten thousand volumes. The simple shape of the house clearly articulates, as well as separates, its two programs: living and working. The residence is a low horizontal form, partially embedded in the earth, that becomes part of the approach to the entire structure. Visitors walk on the roof of the residence to access the partially obscured entrance. From the entry hall, a staircase leads down to the living areas and up to the library, whose axis is perpendicular to that of the residence below.

The residence, which now accommodates the owner and his wife, is a loftlike space broken up by core elements arranged in a simple linear fashion: kitchen, fireplace and chimney, and bathroom. A series of identical vertical window openings wraps around the three exposed sides of the residence, bringing light into the interior at rhythmic intervals.

The library is a double-height space. Occupying a mezzanine suspended over a reading area, the library stacks are protected from any direct exposure to sunlight. By contrast, the lower-level reading space is light-filled and offers views out to the landscape.

The building was constructed with what the architects have called a double-shell system of steel and wood. The materials are structurally independent of each other to allow for their varying degrees of expansion. The exterior shell, a steel frame clad in ¼" weathering-steel plate, seam-welded and ground, was prefabricated as six individual parts and assembled on-site. The result is a seamless, monolithic structure that is highly abstract, without differentiation between vertical and horizontal surfaces and with relatively few clues as to its overall scale.

Site plan

View from northwest

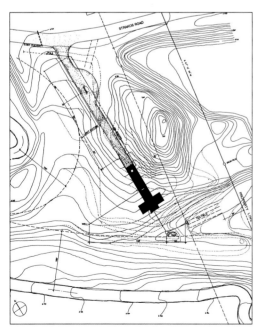

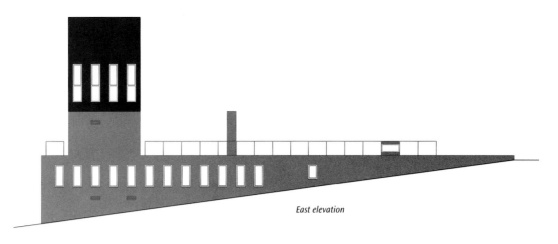

East elevation

View of living areas

1 *Entry hall*
2 *Bedroom*
3 *Living area*
4 *Dining area*
5 *Kitchen*
6 *Reading area and library stacks*

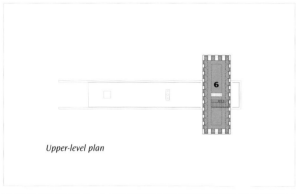

Upper-level plan

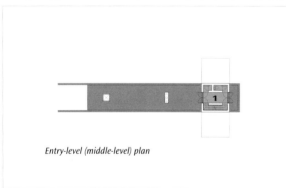

Entry-level (middle-level) plan

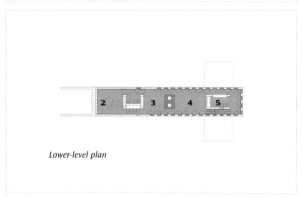

Lower-level plan

Longitudinal section through entry and stairs

Bedroom

Reading area with library stacks above

Designed by Thomas Hanrahan and Victoria Meyers for a single professional man with a sophisticated knowledge of architecture and design, the Holley Loft is a 3,800-square-foot converted industrial-loft space in Manhattan. The principal architectural element is a forty-eight-foot-long glass-and-steel wall, which runs parallel to the length of the loft and delimits the master bedroom and bathroom. This glazed partition, clear glass in parts, sandblasted in others, does not so much separate those areas from the living spaces but rather defines them within a highly fluid spatial structure.

The loft is characterized by a sense of dispersed space and a radical openness. The architects wanted to create a "sense of endless depth" that can be experienced at any moment and from any position in the apartment. They remarked, "The multiple sensations of space and light offered within this project…stress the importance of momentary experiences and fleeting perceptions." Hanrahan's and Meyers's counterpoints of "appearance" and "disappearance" also play a role in the design. The glass-and-steel wall creates visual presence through interactions of its transparent and translucent surfaces. The apartment's solid-wood storage elements, which provide for the loft's major programmatic activities of preparing food, working, and entertaining, serve to contain and organize and thus conceal.

Adaptable to changing circumstances, full-height painted wood panels can be moved to create guest rooms out of an office. As noted by Hanrahan and Meyers, "When they are open, the panels float in the space; closed, they demarcate one room; closed further, two rooms." The overall impression of the loft is one of primal simplicity and studied refinement. "Form is condensed and simplified, and disappears as an obstruction to the comprehension of space," commented the architects.

View of principal living areas

View of kitchen from dining area

Plan
1 Entry
2 Living area
3 Dining area
4 Kitchen
5 Master bedroom
6 Convertible work space/bedroom

View from master bedroom

Movable panels partially closed to create separate rooms

View of master bedroom

Exploded axonometric view

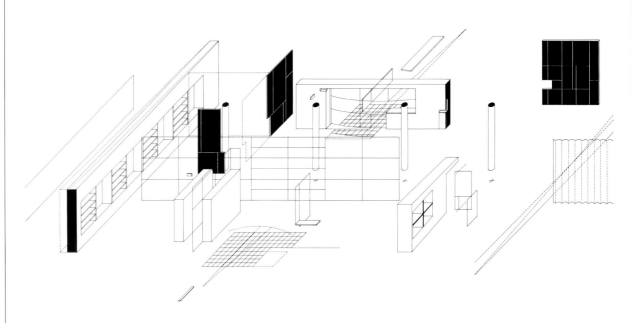

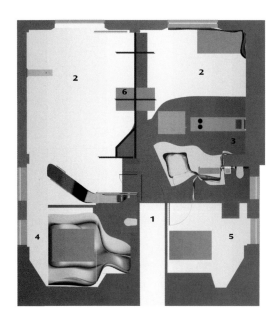

The Ost/Kuttner Apartment in Manhattan was designed by Sulan Kolatan and William Mac Donald for use as a pied-à-terre by a couple whose principal residence is in Virginia and, less frequently, as a corporate apartment for their business visitors. To meet these needs, the architects had to create a flexible design. The 1,600-square-foot space, obtained by combining and reconfiguring two contiguous apartments, offers three sleeping areas with varying degrees of privacy. A paneled partition divides the loftlike space or opens into a grand dining table for entertaining.

Plan
1 Entry
2 Living area
3 Kitchen
4 Master sleeping and bathing area
5 Bedroom
6 Partition/dining table

View from living area toward kitchen and master sleeping and bathing area

Clearly evident in the Ost/Kuttner Apartment is Kolatan's and Mac Donald's fascination for curved, topological forms developed with the aid of sophisticated computer software. They conceived the apartment as a kind of miniature urban setting, with various "sites" available for development. For these sites, the architects created new structures that merge and thereby move beyond traditional domestic forms. They electronically cross-referenced and melded sectional profiles of everyday interior furnishings, such as a bed, sink, sofa, and shelf, to generate forms that are, in their words, "unknown and impossible to preconceive or predict" according to any traditional measure. This process establishes "a chimerical condition between furniture, space, and surface," producing objects and areas that are not

View of partition pivoted to serve as dining table

limited to single programmatic functions.

An example of the resulting structures—which the architects describe as
"synthetic topographies" or "domestic
scapes"—is the overlap between what
might normally be considered a bedroom
and a bathroom. Its forms were seamlessly
cast in integral-color fiberglass, using digital information. The horizontal surface, or
"plateau," of the bed is separated from the
bathtub by a single sheet of glass.

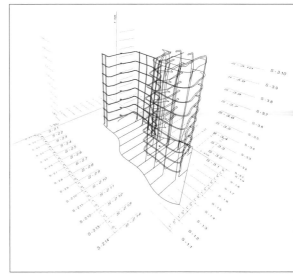

Production diagram of fiberglass for master sleeping and bathing area

Left and above: Master sleeping and bathing area

Designed by Clorindo Testa for a couple, she a business executive and he an artist, the Ghirardo-Kohen House is a reconfiguration and transformation of a large 1920s Tudor house—an example of what the architect has called "Early Nothing style"—in a northern garden suburb of Buenos Aires. In the architect's writings, the design has also been called House on a Slope in reference to its location atop a bluff over the Río de la Plata.

The house cannot be considered to have been "renovated" in a standard sense. Rather, a new architecture has been imported into the space of the preexisting, generating, in Testa's words, "a new proposal in which two periods, two styles, and two opposing architectures coexist." Testa's

interventions are not limited to additions to the existing structures. Rather, like Gordon Matta-Clark's artworks, a new condition is created by judicious removals. In the Ghirardo-Kohen House, interior walls have been literally deconstructed by demolition or incision, and the cellular volumes they defined have been opened up. Lightweight partitions now slide through what was formerly a series of formal rooms, establishing their own geometric patterns.

In contrast to the excisions are the additions of discrete new volumes adjacent to the house: an opaque four-sided structure houses two offices and a library; glass and steel create a crystalline solarium. New architectural surfaces have also been introduced as landscape elements, trans-

forming and intensifying the house's relationship to its environment: a skewed platform extends the house's original vaulted terrace; a swimming pool is cantilevered from the house over the steep hillside, supported by a concrete tree that seems to grow from the slope itself.

Ground-floor and site plan
1 *Entry*
2 *Living area*
3 *Dining area*
4 *Kitchen*
5 *Work space/library*
6 *Solarium*
7 *Terrace*
8 *Pool*

View of work-space/library addition with renovated house in background

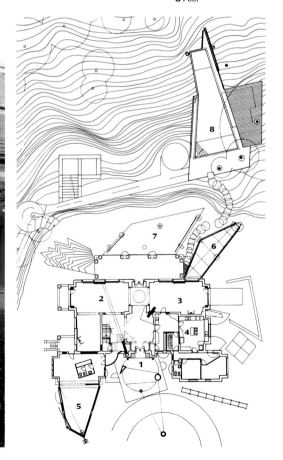

View of solarium and pool

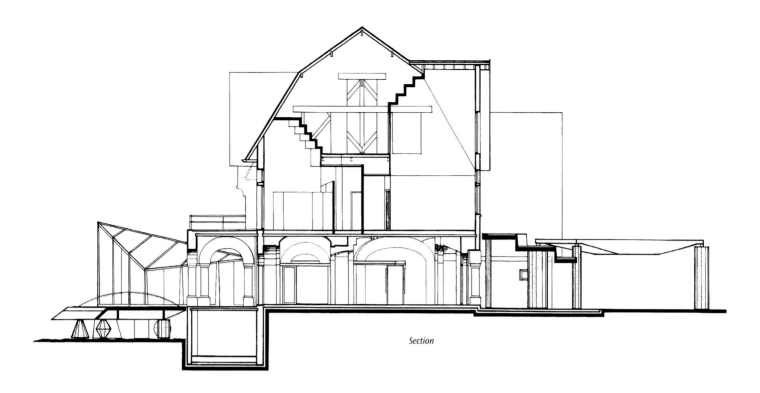

Section

View of solarium and renovated house

View of terrace, renovated house, and solarium

View of main living areas with sliding screens

View of stairs and sliding screens

The M House was designed by Kazuyo Sejima and Ryue Nishizawa as a residence and workplace for a couple. In addition to its more typical programmatic elements, including a living room and kitchen and dining area, the house has work spaces for both husband and wife, a traditional tatami room for guests, and a large space for entertaining. Three bedrooms are intended to accommodate the couple, guests, and, eventually, children.

The house lies in a very desirable, yet densely populated, area in the center of Tokyo. Since many of the houses are not set back from the street, the neighborhood is one of "permanently drawn curtains and high fences," according to the architects. In order to open the M House up to the environment while also maintaining a certain distance from the street, the entire site was excavated to one level below grade. Four double-height spaces, or "light wells," bring natural light into the lower level of the structure. Three of these include courtyard areas open to the sky, which provide

sheltered outdoor space as well as air and natural light.

Sheathed in perforated metal, which cuts sound transmission, the austere street facade reveals only the entrance and the garage door. Yet a large translucent polycarbonate window to the right of the doors lets light into the central court while maintaining privacy. The perforated metal—which has a fine-grained, tactile quality in keeping with that of the polycarbonate—screens the window, so that it is not apparent from the street. All the other windows of the house face onto the courts. While views out to the world beyond are limited, the presence and motion of other people within the residence becomes quite evident, a common trait in traditional Japanese houses.

The M House not only recalls the historical precedents established by Ludwig Mies van der Rohe's courtyard houses but moves beyond them by responding to the critical changes that have taken place in contemporary culture. Rather than framing

the interior views with structural members, the building's design emphasizes the skin of the building and its ability to mediate experience.

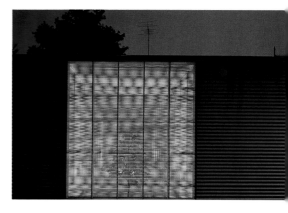

Detail of window onto central light court screened with perforated metal

Principal facade

Detail of central light court at night

1 Entry
2 Bedroom
3 Garage
4 Master bedroom
5 Light court
6 Central light court
7 Kitchen/dining area
8 Living area
9 Music studio
10 Work space

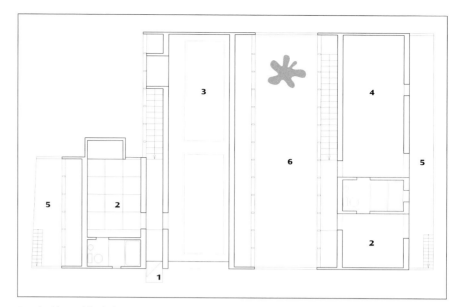

Entry-level (ground-floor) plan

Central light court

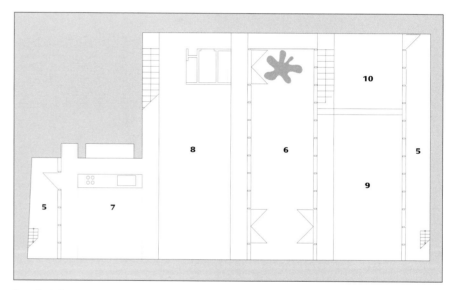

Lower-level plan

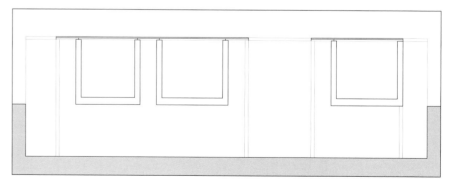

Longitudinal section

View of living area with central light court at left and stairs to entry at right

View of living area with central light court at right

UN Studio/Van Berkel & Bos Möbius House Het Gooi, The Netherlands, 1998

View from north

Designed by Ben van Berkel for a professional couple and their children, the Möbius House derives its name from its conceptual diagram: two intertwined paths that seamlessly integrate program, circulation, and structure. A single-sided surface, the Möbius band is a mathematical model that has become emblematic in contemporary architecture for nonhierarchical, nondialectical ways of thinking. As envisioned by the architect, the house's "diagram liberates architecture from language, interpretation, and signification."

Although its form is not used literally, the Möbius model serves as a reference point throughout the house. The circulation moves in a loop—a "double-locked torus," according to van Berkel—which passes through the more public spaces as well as the couple's offices, the family spaces, and back again. As such, the circulation not only serves a function but also acquires a temporal dimension, reflecting the potential continuity and integration of living and working in the same house. The underlying conceptual diagram is manifest spatially and structurally as well. There is a palpable sense of the twisting of space and material as the architecture seems—from different vantage points—to fold back over onto itself. In a similar way, the relationships between the two main materials, glass and concrete, continuously shift. From one perspective, the glass seems to

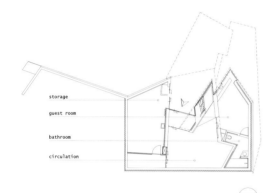

Ground-level plan

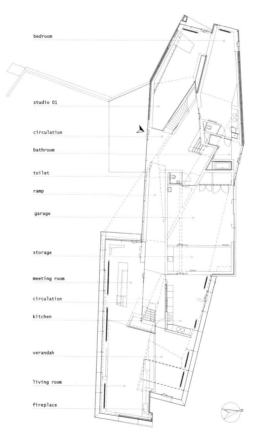

Middle-level plan

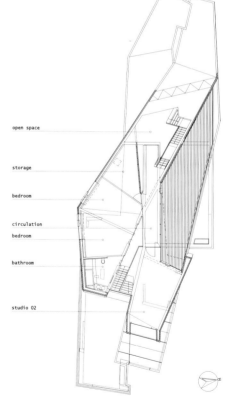

Upper-level plan

be a skin slipped over a concrete house; from another, the building appears to be a glass house framed by concrete members.

Located in a suburban enclave outside of Utrecht, the house's site is comprised of four areas with distinctly different characters. Van Berkel linked the internal organization of the house to these four quadrants, a connection that, he says, "transforms living in the house into a walk in the landscape."

Entry

View of stairs with meeting/dining room at right

View into meeting/dining room from south

View of living area

View from north

View from southeast

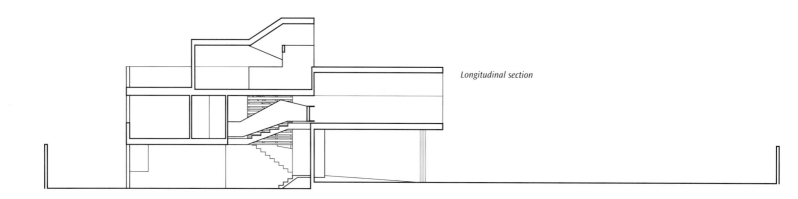

Longitudinal section

View from northwest

Designed by Danelle Guthrie and Tom Buresh as their own work space and home, WorkHouse lies in a part of West Hollywood—a residential area within the Los Angeles sprawl that initially developed as a neighborhood where domestic workers and their families lived. A small cottage still occupies the front part of the site, buffering noise from the busy street. The project's second stage, to date unbuilt, will replace the cottage with a smaller WorkHouse. The completed building is a wood-frame structure rising three stories. Living areas, kitchen, and required covered parking are on the ground level; an architectural studio and child's bedroom are on the second level, with the master bedroom and roof deck on the third.

The house's principal materials are plywood, used for walls and floor, and polycarbonate panels, in the studio. The translucency of the latter produces what the architects have called "a state of continuous flux dependent on the condition of the light at the moment and the position of the observer." That Guthrie and Buresh put issues of the private and the public into play in their design is of particular relevance in an area of increasing housing density. They believe that the "visually shared

Living area and stairs

Stairs at mid-level

spaces between adjacent buildings challenge the expected psychological opacity of the property line, while the translucent membrane of the side elevations preserves the necessary privacy." Inside the house, staggered levels and various methods of screening split spaces devoted to working from those for living. On the second floor, a windowed bathroom orients a typically private space toward public view.

While the WorkHouse project's incorporation of two houses on one plot relates to many economic and cultural changes at play in Southern California, the design of the larger house itself reflects a number of the region's iconic and most influential projects. The way in which the translucent panels lightly enclose the volume of space recalls the lightweight membrane of Charles and Ray Eames's own house of 1945–49 in the Pacific Palisades (fig. 39). Moreover, the inventive deployment of low-cost construction techniques and materials—concrete, off-the-shelf metal windows, and wood-framed glass doors are also used—recalls Rudolph Schindler's Schindler/Chase House in Hollywood (1921–22). The architects see their design as a result of the friction between "the site and the script," which might be described as a theory of practice capable of encompassing on the one hand the pragmatic exigencies of site, history, economy, and government regulation and on the other the idealized vision of modern life in Southern California.

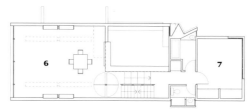

Third-floor plan

1 *Entry*
2 *Carport*
3 *Living area*
4 *Kitchen/dining area*
5 *Proposed structure*
6 *Work space*
7 *Bedroom*
8 *Master bedroom*
9 *Terrace*

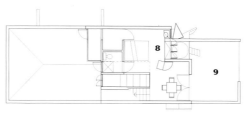

Second-floor plan

View of master bedroom

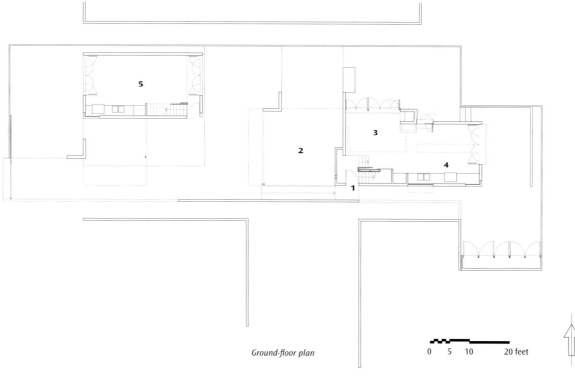

Ground-floor plan

0   5   10   20 feet

Work space

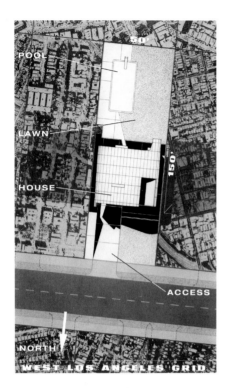

Site plan

*View of house and pool from south.
Computer-generated image*

Neil M. Denari designed the Massey House as a home and graphic-design studio for a young couple. The three-bedroom, unbuilt house was designed to replace a 1950s developer house, one of the thousands of such residences forming what the architect has called the "endless fields of postwar housing in Los Angeles." Noting the difficulties of designing a house for this milieu, Denari wished to inject variation and deformation into the uniformity, while matching the best aspects of the suburban field. In this sense, the house mirrors those conditions that influenced the design and fueled the rapid spread of the Case Study Program's innovative housing prototypes in postwar Southern California: relatively inexpensive land, mild climate, and receptivity to experimentation.

In plan, the house design reflects the basic structure and amenities of tract housing. Like many of its neighbors in Los Angeles's housing grid, the compact structure will occupy nearly the entire width of the site and will be set back at front and rear to accommodate suburbia's iconic domestic equipment: automobiles and a swimming pool. The principal departure from the standard tract house is seen in section. The excavation of land will create a full level below grade, allowing the volume of a three-story house with the appearance of two stories. From side to side, however, the floor will step up by half levels, connected by a central stair, to create a house with seven levels organized by use into interlocking zones.

The overtly technocratic appearance of the house is an affirmation of Southern California's historical openness to an optimistic faith in progress, yet also a foil to the more traditional profiles of its neighbors. Underscoring what might be called the formal aloofness of the project, the architect has said, "Within an urban milieu that is the subject of countless rehearsals of both angst and ennui, this house sits as an ambivalent figure, committed to the preservation of site typology while internally engaging in an extreme criticism of architectural similitudes."

1 *Master bedroom*
2 *Bedroom*

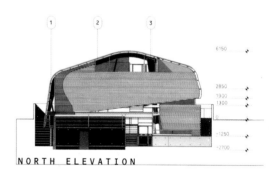

NORTH ELEVATION

UPPER LEVEL PLAN

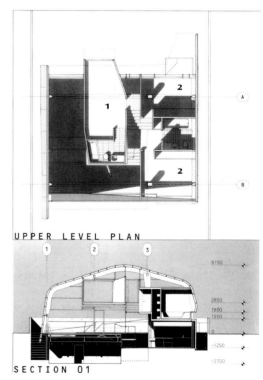

SECTION 01

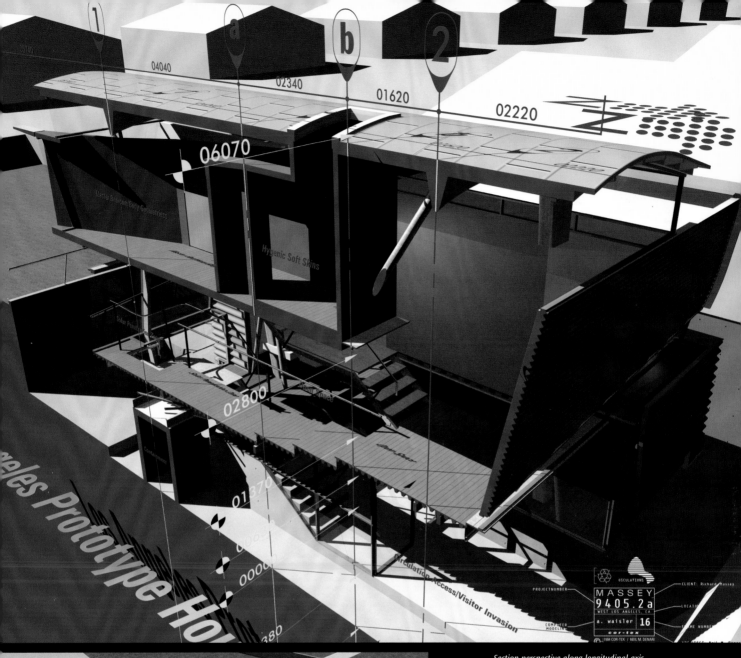

06070

Neuro-Bladder/Body Geometrics

Hygenic Soft Skins

04040

02340

01620

02220

N

02800

01370

geles Prototype Ho...

Circulation Access/Visitor Invasion

OSCULATIONS

MASSEY
9405.2a
WEST LOS ANGELES, CA
a. waisler 16
cor-tex

CLIENT: Richard Massey

PROJECT NUMBER

COMPUTER MODELLER

© 1994 COR-TEX / NEIL M. DENARI

*Section perspective along longitudinal axis.
Computer-generated image*

Aerial view from northwest. Computer-generated image

Living area. Computer-generated image

View of living area from dining area. Computer-generated image

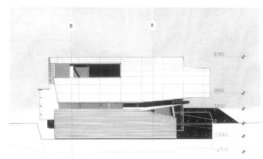

WEST ELEVATION

3 *Living area*
4 *Kitchen*
5 *Dining area*
6 *Work space*

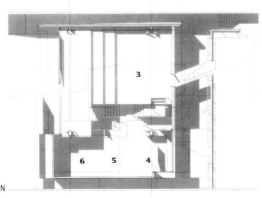

CENTER LEVEL PLAN

Structural x-ray. Computer-generated image

SECTION 02

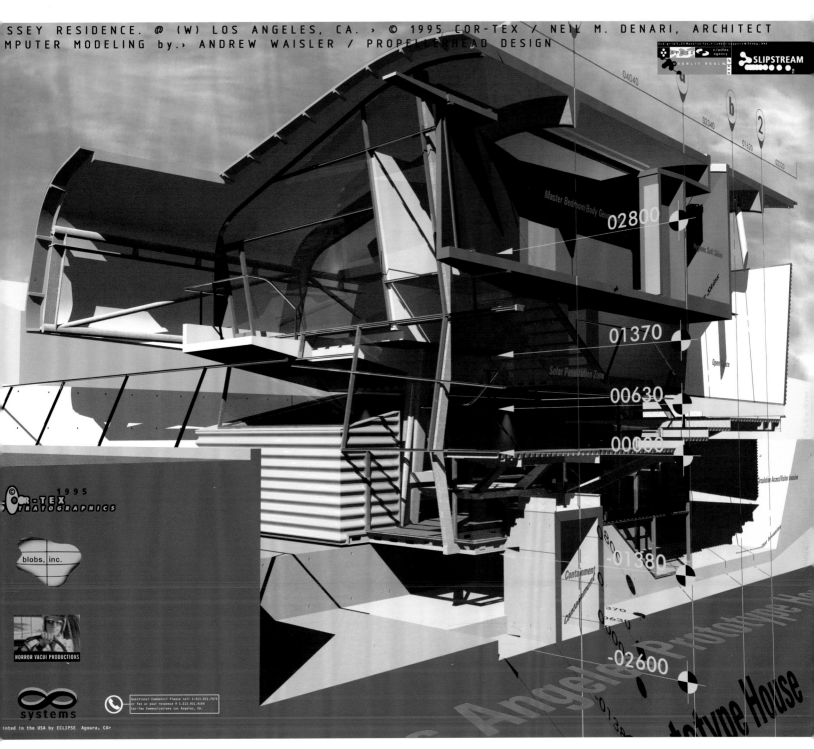

Section perspective along transverse axis. Computer-generated image

Situated atop a hill in the Catskill Mountains, the Y House was designed by Steven Holl as a retreat for a couple and their grown children. Past the entrance areas, the double-height space splits into two branches, one extending west and the other southwest toward the mountain views beyond. Both branches are further extended by porches, and a pool of water lengthens the plan of the northern branch further still.

The house is a meditation on its environment and on natural phenomena. In the words of the architect, "The slow passing of time from early morning to sunset is to be a primary experience in the house, as different areas of the house become activated with the movement of the sun." The house draws from other aspects of the environment as well. The metal roof's various slopes channel rainwater to a cistern north of the house. In winter, southern sun enters the house through the glazing at the ends of the branches, which are protected from summer sun by the deep porches.

Within the house, two spatial dialectics are at play: public/private and day-active/night-sleep. A loftlike, two-story structure would have solved many of these essential issues in a commonplace fashion. However, Holl proposed a "sectional flip of public/private or day/night zones to animate the spaces and their activities." In other words, the public space of the kitchen and dining area, on the ground floor of the southern branch, flows upward to the living room on the upper level of the opposite branch. Similarly, the sleeping rooms jump from the ground floor of the northern branch to the upper level of the southern. The result is a dynamic composition, particularly at the double-height junction of the two wings. The parents' and children's sleeping rooms are not only distinct from the more public spaces but are isolated from each other. As the public spaces extend throughout the house, a sense of spatial continuity is achieved, particularly on the upper level, where the views to the exterior are so dominant.

Diagrammatic sketch of private (night) and public (day) spaces. Watercolor

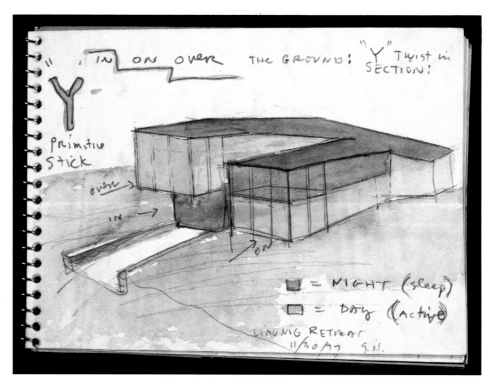

Construction view from southwest

Construction view from northwest

Sketch of stairs. Watercolor

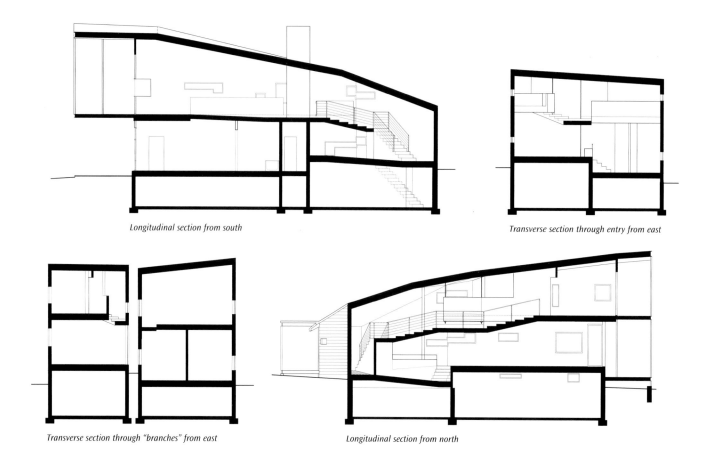

Longitudinal section from south

Transverse section through entry from east

Transverse section through "branches" from east

Longitudinal section from north

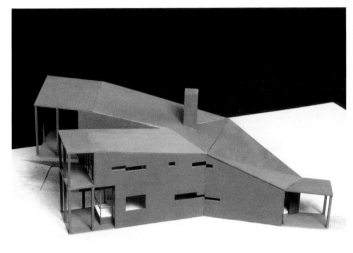

Model from south

Model from east

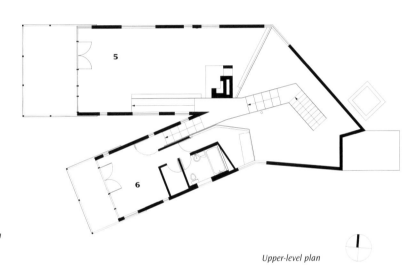

1 *Entry*
2 *Bedroom*
3 *Kitchen/dining area*
4 *Reflecting pool*
5 *Living area*
6 *Master bedroom*

Upper-level plan

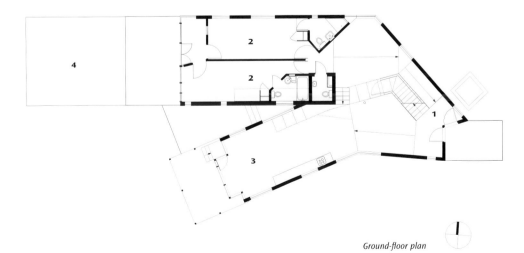

Ground-floor plan

Project Information

Shigeru Ban, Tokyo

Curtain Wall House (pp. 72–75)

Location: Tokyo, Japan
Design: 1993–94
Construction: 1994–95
Total size of project: 179 square meters
Size of ground floor: 75 square meters
Principal structural system: Steel frame
Principal materials: Steel, aluminum, glass, and waterproofed polyester

Clients: Takashi and Yoshiko Tsurimaki
Design team: Shigeru Ban, Shigeru Hiraki, and Yoko Nakagawa
Structural engineer: Hoshino Architect & Engineer
Contractor: Heisei Kensetsu

Michael Bell, Houston

Glass House @ 2° (pp. 64–67)

Location: Houston, Texas
Design: 1999
Construction: 1999–projected completion 2000
Total size: 900 square feet; 5,000-square-foot lot
Size of ground floor: 900 square feet
Principal structural system: Steel frame
Principal materials: Glass, aluminum, and steel

Client: The Fifth Ward Community Redevelopment Corporation, Houston
Design team: Michael Bell, John Mueller, and Todd Vanvarick
Contractor: The Fifth Ward Community Redevelopment Corporation
Climate-control consultant: Keith A.C.

Preston Scott Cohen, Boston

Torus House (pp. 104–07)

Location: Old Chatham, New York
Design: 1998–99
Construction: Projected completion 2001
Total size: 3,104 square feet
Size of ground floor: 912 square feet

Principal structural system: Concrete foundation with steel and wood frame
Principal materials: Concrete, steel, fiberglass, wood, and plywood panels

Client: Eric Wolf
Design team: Preston Scott Cohen, Alexandra Barker, Chris Hoxie, and Eric Olsen
Contractors: d.h.e. Company, Inc., New York; and EEE, Inc., Old Chatham
Landscape design: Andrew Grossman, Seekonk
CAM/three-dimensional printing: Darell Fields

Neil M. Denari, Los Angeles

Massey House (pp. 136–39)

Location: Los Angeles, California
Design: 1994
Construction: Unbuilt
Total size: 3,000 square feet
Size of ground floor: 1,650 square feet
Principal structural system: Steel frame on concrete foundation
Principal materials: Corrugated enameled steel sheet, aluminum, and glass curtain wall

Client: Richard Massey
Design team: Neil M. Denari and Andrew Waisler with Masao Yahagi and Yutaka Matsumoto

Diller + Scofidio, New York

Slow House (pp. 52–55)

Location: Long Island, New York
Design: 1990
Construction: Begun 1991 (subsequently stopped)
Total size: 3,200 square feet
Size of ground floor: 1,700 square feet
Principal structural system: Stressed skin over twenty-seven vertical bents
Principal materials: Plywood and wood

Client: Koji Itakura
Architects: Elizabeth Diller and Ricardo Scofidio

Design team: Victor Wong and Peter Burns
Structural engineer: Ron Mayrbaurl, Weidlinger and Associates
Contractor: David White

Winka Dubbeldam, Archi-Tectonics, New York

Millbrook Residence (pp. 40–43)

Location: Millbrook, New York
Design: 1997
Construction: Unbuilt
Total size: 3,500 square feet; 34-acre site
Size of ground floor: 1,374 square feet
Principal structural system: Cast-in-place concrete with lightweight steel framework
Principal materials: Concrete, steel, glass, aluminum, and fiberglass

Clients: Peter and Cheryl Johns
Design team: Winka Dubbeldam, Julie Schurtz, Joachim Karelse, Fleur Swildens, Roemer Pierik, Maia Small, Stephen Roe, and Thomas Wang
Structural engineer: Guy Nordenson and Associates
Landscape design: Archi-Tectonics

Farjadi Farjadi Architects, London

BV House (pp. 88–91)

Location: Ribble Valley, Lancashire, England
Design: July 1997 (competition proposal)
Construction: 1998–projected completion 1999
Total size: 500 square meters
Size of ground floor: 315 square meters
Principal structural system: Timber and steel frame structure on concrete foundation and slab
Principal materials: Timber, steel, concrete, thatch, aluminum, glass, and polymerized asphalt

Architects: Homa Farjadi and Sima Farjadi
Design team: Martin Bohler, Chris Lee, Zachary Hinchcliff, and Kathy Wright

Construction consultant: Hugh Cullum
Lighting consultant: Mathias Reese
Structural engineers: Jane Wernick and
    Jonathan Latham, Ove Arup & Partners
Mechanical and electrical engineers and
    climate-control consultant: Richard
    Shennan and Will Potter, Fulcrum
    Consultants
Quantity surveyor: Tim Jupp,
    De Leewe Jupp
Contractor: Andrew Branson, Brockhall
    Village
Landscape designer: Farjadi Farjadi
    Architects
Computer graphics: Tony Jones

Xaveer de Geyter
Architectenbureau, Antwerp
House in Brasschaat (pp. 96–99)

Location: Brasschaat, Belgium
Design: 1990
Construction: 1991–92
Total size of project: 505 square meters
Size of ground floor: 335 square meters;
    450 square meters with patios
Principal structural system: Hybrid steel
    and concrete
Principal materials: Concrete, brick, steel,
    prefabricated concrete panels, glass,
    and anodized aluminum panels

Architect: Xaveer de Geyter
Design team: Piet Crevits and Alain
    de Backer
Structural engineer: Jeroen Thomas
Contractor: Goedleven N.V.
Landscape designer: Yves Brunier

Guthrie + Buresh Architects,
Los Angeles
WorkHouse (pp. 132–35)

Location: Los Angeles, California
Design: 1993–94
Construction: 1995–96
Total size: 1,800 square feet
Size of ground floor: 600 square feet
Principal structural system: Wood frame
Principal materials: Plywood, translucent
    polycarbonate panels, cement plaster,
    and concrete

Clients: Danelle Guthrie, Tom Buresh, and
    Ryan Buresh
Architects: Guthrie and Tom Buresh
Design team: Dave Maynard, Mike
    Ferguson, Adam Woltag, and Josh
    Coggeshall
Contractors: RAC Construction; Thomasson
    & Associates; and Guthrie and Buresh
Landscape design: Guthrie and Buresh

Thomas Hanrahan and
Victoria Meyers, Architects,
New York
Holley Loft (pp. 112–15)

Location: Manhattan, New York
Design: 1994
Construction: 1995
Total size: 3,800 square feet
Principal structural system: Existing steel
    frame and terra-cotta slab
Principal materials: Cold-rolled steel,
    maple plywood, clear and sandblasted
    glass, limestone, and plaster

Client: Steven Holley
Design team: Thomas Hanrahan, Victoria
    Meyers, Martha Coleman, Guy Maxwell,
    and James Slade
Mechanical engineer: M. Rubiano, P.C.
Contractor: Jauda Construction
Steel fabricator: Scott Enge, E-Fabrications
Model fabricators: Kevin Lee and
    David Teeple

Hariri & Hariri, New York
The Digital House (pp. 56–59)

Location: A two-acre suburban lot
Design: 1998
Construction: Unbuilt project
Total size: 3,200 square feet
Size of ground floor: 570 square feet;
    3,000 square feet of exterior terraces
    and ramps
Principal structural system: Steel frame
Principal materials: Lightweight steel
    frame units clad in various metals and
    active-liquid-crystal display windows

Client: Sponsored by *House Beautiful*
    magazine as part of its House for the
    Next Millennium series

Architects: Gisue Hariri and Mojgan Hariri
Design team: Karin Mousson
Walk-through animation: John Bennett
    and Gustavo Bonevardi, Proun
    Space Studio
Animation narration and voice:
    John Brehm
LCD-technology engineer: Mark
    Borstelmann, LCD Planar Optics
Model fabricator: Nadya Liebich

Herzog & de Meuron, Basel
Kramlich Residence and Media
Collection (pp. 48–51)

Location: Napa Valley, California
Design: 1997–98
Construction: 1999–projected
    completion 2000
Total size: 20,800 square feet
Size of ground floor: 5,900 square feet
Principal structural system: Cast-in-place
    concrete, steel beams, and decking
Principal materials: Concrete, steel,
    and glass

Clients: Richard and Pamela Kramlich
Architects: Jacques Herzog and Pierre
    de Meuron
Design team: Jean-Frédéric Lüscher
    (project architect), Matthew Gribben,
    Katsumi Darbellay, Peter Sigrist, and
    Rita Diniz
Structural engineer: Zucco Fagent
    Associates, Santa Rosa
Electrical planning: Hansen & Slaughter,
    Inc., San Rafael
Construction management: Valley
    Architects, St. Helena; and B. Byland
    and T. Flaherty, partners, Oliver &
    Company, Richmond
General contractor: Oliver & Company
Climate-control planning: Larkin
    Associates, Sebastopol
Landscape consultant: Molly Chappelet,
    St. Helena

Steven Holl Architects,
New York

Y House (pp. 140–43)

Location: Schoharie County, New York
Design: 1998
Construction: 1998–projected
    completion 1999
Total size: 3,500 square feet
Size of ground floor: 1,500 square feet
Principal structural system: Wood and
    steel frame
Principal materials: Wood and steel

Client: Herbert Liaunig
Architect: Steven Holl
Design team: Erik Fenstad Langdalen
    (project architect), Justin Korhammer,
    Yoh Hanaoka, Annette Goderbauer,
    Chris McVoy, Brad Kelley, and
    Jennifer Lee
Architect on site: Peter Liaunig
Structural engineer: Robert Silman
    Associates, P.C.
Lighting designer: L'Observatoire
    International
General contractor: Dick Dougherty
Furniture fabrication: Face Fabrication
Landscape design: Holl

Kolatan/Mac Donald Studio,
New York

Ost/Kuttner Apartment (pp. 116–19)

Location: Manhattan, New York
Design: 1995–96
Construction: 1996–97
Total size: 1,600 square feet
Principal materials: Aluminum-laminated
    plywood, epoxy, concrete, fiberglass,
    cementitious board, and stainless steel

Clients: Beatrix Ost and Ludwig Kuttner
Architects: Sulan Kolatan and William
    Mac Donald
Design team: Erich Schoenenberger
    (project architect), Rebecca Carpenter,
    Natasha Cunningham, Steven Doub,
    Matt Hollis, Philip Palmgren, and
    Patrick Walsh
Structural engineer: Ove Arup and Partners
General contractor: Foundations Design
    International, Inc.

Rem Koolhaas, Office for
Metropolitan Architecture,
Rotterdam

Maison à Bordeaux (pp. 92–95)

Location: Bordeaux, France
Construction: Completed 1998
Total size: 500 square meters (main house)
Principal structural system: Concrete and
    steel
Principal materials: Concrete, steel,
    aluminum, and glass

Architects: Rem Koolhaas with Maarten
    van Severen
Design team: Jeanne Gang, Julien Monfort,
    Bill Price, Jeroen Thomas, Yo Tamagata,
    Chris Dondorp, Erik Schotte, and
    Vincent Costes
Engineers: Cecil Balmond and Robert
    Pugh, Ove Arup & Partners
Facade consultant: Robert-Jan van Santen
Hydraulics consultant: Gerard
    Couillandeau
Coordination and technical assistant:
    Michel Régaud
Interiors consultant: Petra Blaisse
Fitted-furnishing and mobile-platform
    designers: Maarten van Severen and
    Raf de Preter
Bookcase designer: Vincent de Rijk

Frank Lupo/Daniel Rowen,
Architects, New York

Lipschutz/Jones Apartment (pp. 44–47)

Location: Manhattan, New York
Design: 1987
Construction: 1988
Total size: 1,500 square feet
Principal structural system: Wood and
    metal framing systems
Principal materials: Maple, slate, marble,
    granite, glass block, frosted glass
    panels, stainless steel, aluminum plate,
    and Pirelli rubber

Clients: William Lipschutz and
    Lynnelle Jones
Design team: Frank Lupo, Daniel Rowen,
    Alissa Bucher, and Richard Blender
Structural engineer: Ed Messina,
    Severud Associates

Mechanical engineers: Ambrosino DePinto
    & Schmieder
Contractor: Gordon Construction

Michael Maltzan Architecture,
Los Angeles

Hergott Shepard Residence (pp. 76–79)

Location: Beverly Hills, Los Angeles,
    California
Design: 1996–97
Construction: 1997–99
Principal structural system: Wood and
    steel frame
Principal materials: Zinc panels
    (Rheinzine), plaster, Douglas fir, and
    English sandstone

Clients: Alan Hergott and Curt Shepard
Architect: Michael Maltzan
Design team: Chris Mehren, Melanie
    McArtor, Jeanette Fabry, Paul Lee, and
    Mike Soriano
Structural consultant: William K. Koh &
    Associates
Civil-engineering consultant: Bob Newlon
    & Associates
Mechanical and plumbing consultant:
    Innovative Engineering Group, Inc.
Electrical consultant: Nikolakopoulos &
    Associates
Lighting consultant: Lam Partners, Inc.
Kitchen consultant: Bulthaup (LA) Inc.
Contractor: McCoy Construction
Audio and video: Micheal's Co.
Surveyor: M & M & Co.
Landscape design: Jay Griffith, Inc.
Geotechnical and soils engineer:
    The J. Byer Group
Soils (shoring) consultant: Cefali &
    Associates

Francois de Menil, Architect,
New York

Shorthand House (pp. 80–83)

Location: Houston, Texas
Design: 1996
Construction: 1996–97
Total size: 3,480 square feet
Size of ground floor: 1,630 square feet
(without garage)
Principal structural system: Concrete slab
on piers and wood frame
Principal materials: Concrete, wood,
stucco, and maple

Client: Elsian Cozens
Design team: Francois de Menil, James
Moustafellos (project architect),
Vicken Arslanian, John Blackmon,
Stephen Mullins, Amy Nowacki, and
Lavinia Pana
Structural engineer: Guy Nordenson
Mechanical engineers: Mahadev Raman
and Colm Hogan, Ove Arup & Partners
Contractor: Kurt Lobprise, president,
Builders West, Inc., Houston
Construction consultant: Craig Hughes,
president, Hughes Building & Design,
Inc., Houston
Landscape designer: William Hartman,
project manager, SLA Studio Land, Inc.,
Houston

MVRDV, Rotterdam

Two Houses on Borneo Sporenburg
(pp. 60–63)

Borneo Sporenburg-12
Location: Amsterdam, The Netherlands
Design: 1997–98
Construction: Projected completion 1999
Total size: 200 square meters
Size of ground floor: 43 square meters

Architects: Winy Maas, Jacob van Rijs, and
Nathalie de Vries with Arno van der
Mark, artist
Design team: Joost Glissenaar, Bart Spee,
Alex Brouwer, and Arno van der Mark,
artist
Structural engineer: Pieters Bouwtechniek,
Haarlem
Climate-control consultant: DGMR, Arnhem

Borneo Sporenburg-18
Location: Amsterdam, The Netherlands
Date of design: 1997–98
Construction dates: 1998–projected
completion 1999
Total size of project: 150 square meters
Size of ground floor: 50 square meters
Principal structural system: Cast-in-place
concrete walls with stabilizing cross
walls and floors
Principal materials: Concrete, glass,
Prodema panels, and aluminum

Clients: C. Wiersema and P. Frölich
Architects: Winy Maas, Jacob van Rijs, and
Nathalie de Vries
Design team: Joost Glissenaar, Bart Spee,
Alex Brouwer, and Frans de Witte
Structural engineer: Pieters Bouwtechniek,
Haarlem
Contractor: Teerenstra, Heiloo
Climate-control consultant: DGMR, Arnhem

SANAA/Kazuyo Sejima, Ryue Nishizawa &
Associates, Tokyo

M House (pp. 124–27)

Location: Tokyo, Japan
Design: 1996
Construction: 1996–97
Total size: 214.53 square meters
Size of ground floor: 112.08 square meters
Principal structural system: Reinforced
concrete and steel frame
Principal materials: Reinforced concrete,
steel, corrugated metal, aluminum,
and polycarbonate panels

Client: T. Matsumoto
Architects: Kazuyo Sejima and Ryue Nishizawa
Design team: Yoshifumi Kojima and
Yoshitaka Tanase
Structural engineers: Sadakazu Yoda and
Yoshio Kimura, ORS Office
Mechanical engineer: Akiko Sano, System
Design Laboratory
Electrical engineers: Kazuhiro Endo and
Nichiei Sekkei
Contractor: Heisei Kensetsu Co.

Joel Sanders, Architect, New York

House for a Bachelor (pp. 100–03)

Location: Minneapolis, Minnesota
Design: 1998
Construction: Unbuilt
Total size: 4,200 square feet
Size of ground floor: 3,100 square feet
Principal structural system: Wood
frame with steel columns and glass
curtain wall
Principal materials: Wood, steel, glass,
stucco, mahogany paneling, and
Astroturf

Design team: Joel Sanders, Claes Appelquist,
Charles Stone, Cedric Cornu, Nicholas
Haagensen, Marc Tsurumaki, Alexandra
Ultsch, and Christine Kolovich
Contractor: Bob Angen, Emerald Builders,
Minneapolis
Landscape design: Joel Sanders, Architect

Scogin Elam and Bray Architects,
Atlanta

64 Wakefield (pp. 84–87)

Location: Atlanta, Georgia
Design: 1995–97
Construction dates: 1996–97
Total size: 3,600 square feet
Size of ground floor: 2,800 square feet
Principal structural system: Wood frame
and cast-in-place reinforced concrete
Principal materials: Wood, stucco, glass,
concrete, and steel

Clients: Mack Scogin and Merrill Elam
Architects: Scogin and Elam
Structural engineer: Palmer Engineering
Company
Lighting designer: Ramon Luminance
Design
General contractor: John Wesley Hammer
Construction Company
Landscape designer: Edward L. Daugherty

Clorindo Testa, Architect,
Santa Fe, Argentina

Ghirardo-Kohen House (pp. 120–23)

Location: Buenos Aires, Argentina
Design: 1992–93
Construction: 1993–94
Date of original house: 1925
Total size: 1,200 square meters; 8,000-square-meter site
Size of ground floor: 700 square meters
Principal structural system: Concrete
Principal materials: Concrete, bricks, ceramic, and plaster

Clients: Alfredo Ghirardo and Nora Kohen
Design team: Clorindo Testa and Juan Fontana
Structural engineer: Del Villar, Curutchet
Electrical engineer: Cantaluppi
Air-conditioning engineer: Wiegandt, Studio
Contractor: SEBADI S.A.
Landscape design: Testa

Bernard Tschumi, New York

The Hague Villa (pp. 68–71)

Location: The Hague, The Netherlands
Design: 1992
Construction: Unbuilt (project built but not as designed)
Total size: 200 square meters
Size of ground floor: 115 square meters
Principal structural system: Concrete frame
Principal materials: Steel, concrete, brick, and glass

Client: Geerlings Vastgoed BV
Design team: Bernard Tschumi and Tomasz Kowalski
Glass-technology consultant: Hugh Dutton

Simon Ungers with
Thomas Kinslow, New York

T-House (pp. 108–11)

Location: Wilton, New York
Design: 1988
Construction: 1989–92
Total size: 2,500 square feet
Size of ground floor: 1,000 square feet
Principal structural system: Steel frame
Principal materials: Steel, weathering-steel plate, and wood

Client: Lawrence Marcelle
Structural engineer: Ryan & Biggs Associates
Contractors: Exterior: STS; interior: Regenerative Building Construction
Climate-control consultant: Alltek

UN Studio/Van Berkel & Bos, Amsterdam

Möbius House (pp. 128–31)

Location: Het Gooi, The Netherlands
Design: 1993
Construction: 1996–98
Total size: approximately 550 square meters
Size of ground floor: 358 square meters
Principal materials: Concrete, glass, and steel

Architect: Ben van Berkel
Design team: Aad Krom (project coordination), Jen Alkema, Casper le Fèvre, Rob Hootsmans, Matthias Blass, Marc Dijkman, Remco Bruggink, Tycho Soffree, Harm Wassink, and Giovanni Tedesco
Technical consultants: ABT, Velp; and Heijckmann Bouwadviesbureau, Huissen
Interior design: Van Berkel, Hans Kuyvenhoven, Jen Alkema, and Matthias Blass
Contractor: Kemmeren Bouw, b.v., Aalsmeer
Landscape designer: West 8 Landscape Architects, Rotterdam

Credits

Trustees of The Museum of Modern Art